THE EFFECTS OF TRANSACTION COSTS ON COMMUNITY FOREST MANAGEMENT IN UGANDA

Joseph Wasswa-Matovu

Organisation for Social Science Research
in Eastern and Southern Africa (OSSREA)

© 2010 Organisation for Social Science Research in Eastern and Southern Africa (OSSREA)

All rights reserved.

Published in Ethiopia

ISBN: 978-999444-55-59-21

Organisation for Social Science Research in
Eastern and Southern Africa (OSSREA)
P.O. Box 31971
Addis Ababa, Ethiopia
E-mail: ossrea@ethionet.et
Web site: http//www.ossrea.net

OSSREA acknowledges the support of the Swedish International Development Co-operation Agency (Sida/SAREC), Norwegian Agency for Development Co-operation (NORAD), and The Netherlands' Ministry of Foreign Affairs.

TABLE OF CONTENTS

	Executive Summary	iv
	List of Acronyms	xi
1.	**Background**	
2.	Concepts and Characterization of Community Forestry	6
3.	Methodology	25
4.	Study Results	31
5.	Conclusion and Recommendation	61
	References	68

EXECUTIVE SUMMARY

Introduction

Uganda has 4.9 million hectares of forest resources, which cover 24 per cent of the land area. Most of these forests resources have been controlled under customary tenure without clear management schemes. However, in recent years Collaborative Forest Management (CFM) has come to see local communities cooperating with government or its agencies in the management of gazetted forest reserves. Organized in Communal Land Associations (CLA), community members enter into a Memoranda of Understanding/Agreement with the National Forestry Authority (NFA) to manage part or whole of a gazetted forest reserve.

In Budongo Sub-county in Masindi District (Western Uganda), a Community Based Organization (CBO), the Budongo Community Development Organization (BUCODO) working with the NFA has piloted CLAs as institutions through which communities can manage their forest resources. However, presently little empirical evidence exists that points to the effects transaction costs in Community Forestry (CF) play in retarding the success of such initiatives. Equally, the shifting of central government control over natural resource management to communities, while *a priori* is argued to lead to improvements in the condition of forest resources; the distribution of transaction costs across various sub-groups of resource users is generally not incorporated into an economic analysis of participatory forest management, leading to failure of communal efforts.

For households in Budongo Sub-county, where BUCODO did pilot CLAs, this study sought to:

1. Examine the level of transaction costs households faced in community forestry, and to gauge their effects on community forestry initiatives; and
2. Determine the distribution of community forestry transaction costs across households with diverse socio-economic characteristics and gauge their effects on community forestry initiatives.

Key research questions in this regard were:

1. What level of transaction costs do households face in Community Forestry and what effect do they have on community forestry initiatives? and
2. How significant are transaction costs as a proportion of total resource benefits and appropriation costs among households with different socio-economic attributes? What does this imply for community forestry initiatives?

Methodology

Primary data on household level variables and the use and management of community forests was collected among household heads and/or other competent household members in three parishes in Budongo Sub-County. A stratified random sample of households was drawn from a census list of village households. This sampling method sought to categorise households into three ranks, i.e. poor, middle wealth and rich, based on land size holding. Poor households were taken to own 1 or less acres, middle-wealth households to own between 1 and 5 acres, and rich households to own 5 or more acres. A total of 258 households were sampled.

Although land size holding formed the basis for sampling, households were also assessed on their other socio-economic characteristics (household value holdings of farm implements, livestock, and household use and consumer-oriented assets) in order to tease out relations between these characteristics and other variables of interest in the study (e.g. participation in community forestry, levels of transaction costs incurred in community forestry, etc).

Questions on transaction costs focused on time household members spent participating in various community forestry activities (attending village forestry meetings, monitoring others' forest resource use and management practices, and attending conflict resolution meetings). Data was also collected on the amount of time household members spent in collecting, processing and transporting a unit of forest products from Community Forests (CFs) to house, rural hourly wages in agriculture, the costs and economic life of farm implements, etc.

Based on these data, estimates of resource appropriation costs, transaction costs and value of benefits households derived from community forests were computed. Using costs and benefits thus computed, net benefits from community forestry were calculated for households with different socio-economic characteristics and an evaluation made on their effects on community forestry initiatives in the study areas.

Open-ended discussions with groups of forest users, NFA and BUCODO officials provided additional information (i.e. forest users' patterns of resource extraction and management, village level decision-making processes for community forestry, the nature of transaction costs faced in community forestry and institutional and legal constraints). This was used to triangulate some of the information provided by respondents, with bivariate analysis methods used to establish relationships between variables using SPSS.

Research Findings

Survey Population

Households averaged 5.9 persons, with the majority of respondents claiming to have been born in the localities where they resided, or being long-standing migrants in them. Almost all respondents were heads of households with a mean age of 39 (males) and 36 (females), with close to half belonging to ethnic groups that were not indigenous to the study areas. The majority of respondents also had basic (primary) and secondary education.

Household Asset Ownership

Close to half of households had at their disposal land holdings above 1 acre, with those with less, accessing land through land rental and lease markets, or as squatters. Customary tenure was the dominant land tenure system. On average, household wealth held in livestock, farm implements and other household use/consumer-oriented assets amounted to Uganda shillings 86,528 (US$ 53.41), 48,529 (US $30) and 238,350 (US $147) respectively.

Households' Farm and Non-farm activities

All households diversified their productive activities by engaging in both farm (crop cultivation and livestock rearing) and non farm (trading/shop keeping, craftwork, brick-making, the dispensing of herbal medicines, brewing, sales of agricultural and non-agricultural labour within and outside the community) activities. The more economically disadvantaged households more likely to diversify their productive activities.

Household Use of Community Forests

Firewood and water were the key forest products households procured from community forests, although medicinal/herbal plants, edible plants and livestock feeds were the other important forest products. Households' needs for timber were hardly met from community forests, with the harvesting of this product facing severe quantity and maturity restrictions, or outright bans.

Economic Importance of Community Forests to Households

Households visited community forests more often to extract water and firewood resources. Land-constrained households were more likely to visit community forests to procure food and firewood products and to encroach on the forests by engaging in charcoal burning and crop cultivation. On the other hand, households rich in farm implements benefited more from community forests as they could more effectively extract threshold levels of forestry resources, face less resource extraction times, and visit the forest more frequently.

Money Values of Community Forest Products to Households

Households on average extracted Ugandan shilling 672 (US$ 0.42) and 2133 (US$ 1.32) worth of water and firewood a week. These values did not greatly differ among households with different socio-economic characteristics. Especially for firewood, these low valves suggested that households faced few economic incentives (of a monetary kind) to not use their community forest resources sustainably.

Resource Appropriation Costs

On average households expended approximately Ugandan shillings 506 (US$ 0.31) in cost of tools weekly to extract forest resources. Overall, poor (rich) households faced lower (higher) tools appropriation costs as they held few (more) productive assets or tools. Also, a strong relation existed between a household's wealth position and resource appropriation costs, which suggested that while the harvesting of key forest resources (i.e. water and firewood) may have required the use of simple tools, resource collecting, processing and transportation was time-intensive for some economically marginal households.

Rule Design and Households' Members' Participation in Community Forestry

Respondents in their majorities considered oversight functions in forests as the responsibility of the NFA, even as they understood community forestry rules to emanate from cooperative and participatory community governance institutions, such as Local Council (LCs), CLA and the NFA. The majority of respondents were also satisfied with the way rules were designed, with complaints revolving around the domination of deliberations by local leaders/elites and forestry officials, and discriminative practices against women and disabled persons.

The majority of respondents claimed that they and/or members of their households actively participated in community forestry activities. For those reporting non-participation, corruption and illegal practices in forests (sanctioned by forestry officials and politicians) such as timber felling, charcoal burning, crop cultivation and the earmarking of degraded forests for CFM- all dampened their enthusiasm for community forestry. Also, disproportionately more high income households participated in the different community forestry activities, while disproportionately more poor households were likely to commit less time to community forestry activities.

Transaction and Resource Appropriation Costs and Household Wealth Ranks

For those households that had members who actually participated in community forestry activities, almost 90 per cent faced weekly transaction costs in community forestry, not exceeding Ugandan shillings 2200 (US$ 1.36). Richer households faced higher transaction costs in community forestry compared to middle wealth and poor households as richer households had members who spent more time in community forestry. On the other hand, poor households faced higher appropriation costs because of their lower asset bases (especially productive tools), whose use values were quickly amortized over time.

Value of Benefits Households Accrue from Community Forests.

Rich households benefited more from the extraction of the key resources (water and firewood) from community forests compared to their middle income and poor counterparts. The possession of threshold levels of tools and the greater frequency with which richer households extracted community forest products explained why richer households benefited more from community forests.

Transaction Costs as a share of Appropriation Costs and Total Benefits

Transaction costs as a share of total resource appropriation costs were higher for rich and middle income households than for poor households by a factor of 3; implying that when transaction costs in community forestry were evaluated as a share of the costs of forests resources extraction, wealthier households share a heavier burden of these costs than their poorer counterparts. On the other hand, transaction costs as a share of total value of benefits revealed no discernable patterns across different households. This implied that when transaction costs in community forestry are factored into the benefits households derived from their community forests, all households obtained the same benefits–given the costs incurred in community forestry.

Household Net Benefits from Community Forestry.

Overall, all households suffered 0 or negative net benefits from community forestry initiatives in the study areas. The implication is that when transaction costs of community forestry are evaluated in terms of their benefits to households, an incentive existed for households to engage in greater resource appropriations than in those activities that ensured sustainable resource use (i.e. those activities that underpin CFM).

Conclusion and Recommendation

When transaction costs in community forestry are evaluated as the difference of their share in the benefits and costs of resource appropriation from community forests, households in the study areas face few incentives to engage in community forestry. This conclusion emanates from the fact that:

1) The low state of social capital in the study areas hinders participation in community forestry; undermines the authority of traditional leaders to mobilize for collective action, and invariably raises transaction costs;

2) Poverty and a lack of opportunities to diversify income sources, which creates incentives for households to engage in unsustainable community forest use and management practices such as crop cultivation and charcoal burning;

3) The lack of incentives for community forestry that flow from the high forest resource appropriation costs because some households

lack threshold levels of assets (tools) to effectively harvest, process and transport community forest resources to house;

4) Disincentives households face to participate in community forestry on account of corrupt and illegal practices by forestry officials and politicians, discriminatory practices against marginal groups and the domination of community forestry initiatives by local leaders and community elites;

5) The failure of CLAs to be fully democratic and accountable;

6) The low level of monetary values households derive from community forest products; and

7) Institutional and policy bottlenecks around community forestry initiatives.

Efforts to reorient community forestry initiatives towards a truly benefit-oriented and equitable model of people's participation in forest management are proposed here to require:

1) Paying more attention to operationalizing guidelines for forest benefit sharing, transfer of property rights, registration of CLAs and declaration of Community Forests;

2) The capacity of state agencies to be built up by increasing manpower and other resources to the agencies and the operationalization of other more inclusive forums for all community members to discuss issues around CFM as a counter to some of the inequities of power and voice inherent in CFM initiatives conceived under the rubric of CLAs;

3) Advocacy spearheaded by CBOs such as BUCODO) to sensitize skeptical forest resource managers, like the NFA, about the need to transfer property rights and control of forest resources to communities by demonstrating to them that communities are capable of managing these resources;

4) Sufficient and user-friendly information to be packaged and disseminated to forest dependent communities on CFM Agreements specifying community members' commitments to avoid their being manipulated by CLA leaders;

5) BUCODO to streamline gender and equity issues in CFM Agreements, CLAs and community forestry activities;

6) The greater development of grassroots networks of civil societies/NGOs/CBOs that work to build the assets (both social and physical) of economically marginal households and individuals; and

7) Advocacy work to be stepped up at policy level to influence government on good governance issues in the forest sector, the role

of both the political and civil leadership, accountability of responsible institutions, and collaborative forest management.

In conclusion, measures that seek to garner the participation of communities in CFM, but underplay the importance of well functioning institutions (i.e. rules and regulations underpinning CFM, local and traditional governance structures and their roles in building community social capital, democratic and accountable CLAs, etc.) are bound to fail. The success of CFM initiatives in the study areas therefore calls for measures to strengthen all manner of institutions that promote community cooperation and participation for community forestry, and in particular measures to improve household income and asset bases to lower transaction costs in community forestry.

List of Acronyms

BICHRP	BUCODO Integrated Conservation and Reproductive Health Project
BUCCOMA	Community Based Commercial Cultivation of Medicinal Plants
BUCODO	Budongo Community Development Organization
CAFA	Conalum Agro-forestry Farmers Association
CBO	Community Based Organization
CF	Community Forestry
CFM	Collaborative Forest Management
CLA	Communal Land Association
COs	Community Organizers
CPR	Common Property Resource
DPs	Design Principles
FAO	Food and Agriculture Organization
FECOFUN	Federation of Community Forestry Users of Nepal
FID	Forestry Inspection Division
FSCS	Forest Sector Co-ordination Secretariat
FUGs	Forest User Groups
IDP	Internally Displaced Person
JFM	Joint Forest Management
NAADS	National Agricultural Advisory Services
NFA	National Forest Authority
NGO	Non Governmental Organization
PFM	Participatory Forest Management
POs	People's Organizations
RECOFTC	Regional Community Forestry Training Centre
UK	United Kingdom
UNHS	Uganda National Household Survey
USA	United States of America

Definitions of Key Terms in the Study

Transaction costs in community forestry is the value of the *product* of time spent by household members in community forestry activities (attending meetings of forest resource users, monitoring forest resource use and sanctioning/conflict resolution meetings) and a shadow wage – the rural hourly wage rate, which is taken as a proxy of the opportunity cost of household members' time;

Appropriation costs is the value of the *product* of the amount of time spent in collecting, processing and transporting a unit of forest products from community forest to house and a shadow wage – the rural hourly wage rate, which is taken as a proxy of the opportunity cost of household members' time;

Appropriation costs with tools is the value of appropriation costs plus the amortized value of household production tools; and

Total Benefit value is the *product* of the amounts of forests products households procured from the forests (specifically water and firewood), frequency of harvest and the rural unit price of the products.

1. Background

Uganda has 4.9 million hectares of forest resources, which cover 24 per cent of the land area. The majority of this forest area is woodland (81 per cent), some tropical high forest (19 per cent) and forest plantations (less than 1 per cent) (GoU 2002 4). The basic instruments of state authority over forests are the forest laws[1], which regulate the existence and management of forests, and the Land Act[2], which regulates ownership and use of land upon which forest resources are located. In terms of land ownership, the majority (70 per cent) of the forest area is on private land and the remainder is held in trust by the government for the citizens of Uganda.

The vast majority of private forests are natural woodland whose main commercial value is currently charcoal production; a smaller proportion is tropical high forest, whose main commercial value is hardwood timber. However, these private and public forests offer far more than just commercial value to forest owners, surrounding communities and the national economy. Forests have important spiritual value, provide vital subsistence for many communities and are ultimately important in maintaining an environment that advances development (*ibid.*)

In Uganda, forests have often been controlled under customary ownership without clear management schemes. Under changing national governance systems, such a situation has generally resulted in user rights becoming increasingly unclear and to destructive open-access use. This has especially been detrimental to those with weaker rights, particularly women and the poor, as they rely disproportionately on these resources, yet they lack the means to influence the way they are used and managed. On the other hand however, *formalized and constitutional community forests* have the potential to avoid such problems by providing for democratic management and fair access to the group of users through Participatory Forest Management (PFM).[3]

1.1 Collaborative Forest Management (CFM) in Uganda

Collaborative Forest Management (CFM) is the most known and practiced form of Participatory Forest Management (PFM) in Uganda. It involves local communities co-operating with government to manage gazetted forest reserves. In Uganda, the law requires that local communities organize themselves and register a Community Based Organizations (CBOs) before entering into Memoranda of Understanding/Agreement with the government, i.e. the National Forestry Authority (NFA) in the case of Central Forest Reserves and the District Forest Services in the case of Local Forest Reserves, to manage part or whole of a gazetted forest reserve. The registered CBOs are generally facilitated in their formation by external financing (as in the case of BUCODO) and/or the initiatives of local leaders through local governance structures (i.e. Local Councils) within Uganda's decentralized governance structures. Traditional authority and governance structures are noted to play no role in the formation and/or registering of CBOs.

In the past, the traditional protectionist approach of policing forest reserves in Uganda has not been effective in reducing widespread illegal activities or favored local communities in sharing benefits from protected forest areas (GoU 2001).[4] There has been denial of access to forest resources, insensitive management styles, and a lack of opportunity for communities to voice their concerns[5]. The end result has been the proposal and adoption of Collaborative Forest Management (CFM) initiatives to abate these encumbrances in the use and management of forest resources.

The current 2001 Forestry Policy imposes an imperative on government to promote innovative approaches to community participation in forest management on both government and private forestlands. The intention is to provide a balance between the protectionist approach to forest management and destructive open access forest resource use practices (GoU 2001). Thus, with the promulgation of the 1995 Constitution, new policies and approaches have been devised to improve the legal status and tenure rights for customary land interests in natural resources and reduce the power of the state, thereby placing the onus of fair and responsible usage on local communities.

The Policy puts a strong emphasis on public involvement, especially of forest adjacent communities, and benefit sharing from sustainable forest management, including the application of CFM. It says in part:

> Collaborative Forest Management will define the rights, roles and responsibilities of partners and the basis for sharing benefits from improved management. There will be a specific focus on wide stakeholder participation, collective responsibility and equity and on improving the livelihoods of forest dependent communities (*ibid*).

CFM guidelines include as key objectives of CFM, the rehabilitation of degraded forests, the maintenance of forest reserve boundaries and the regulation of access to forest products, joint law enforcement and public participation in forest management. Further to the development of CFM guidelines is the need for CFM regulations, which provide for the rules and requirements for CFM and pave way for better understanding of the roles and responsibilities of concerned parties.

The CFM process is guided by principles that partners have to adhere to and which include:

- A process approach based on learning by doing – communities as well as forest resource managers learn from one another;
- Meaningful participation and shared analysis – communities getting deeply involved;

- Negotiation and consensus building – exchange of opinion, the give and-take approach;
- Appropriate representation and responsibilities – with due consideration of women, the elderly and other disadvantage groups;
- A supporting legal and policy framework– CFM guidelines;
- Building capacity for change – tolerating one another;
- Long term perspective – starting small and thinking big, forestry enterprises are long term; and
- Transparent communication to attract marginalized stakeholders.

1.2 Policy and Legal Provisions of Community Forests

Community Forests (CFs) are ones where communities registered as legal entities choose to set aside and seek gazettement of a forest on communal land as a Community Forest, which they then manage. In Uganda the management of CFs has three important characteristics:

- A Community Forest has to be formally registered as provided for under Sections 17 - 20 of the National Forest and Tree Planting Act (2003);
- A registered Community Forest requires the formal governance structure of a registered Communal Land Association (CLA), which is provided for under the Land Act 1997. The CLA must have a constitution in place to ensure equitable and accountable management;
- A Community Forest (CF) introduces security of tenure through the opportunity to apply for Certificate of Customary Ownership (a group land title).

The law provides that Community Forests should be managed, maintained and controlled by the members of the registered association. The registered - corporate entity - becomes the owner, manager and key beneficiary of the community forest's resources. The Communal Land Association is obliged to manage the forest resource according to all the environmental laws of Uganda.

Currently, CFM (henceforth referred to as community forestry) in Uganda is implemented by the National Forestry Authority (NFA) in the Lake Shore Range (in Mukono, Rakai districts), the Budongo Ecosystem Range (in Masindi district) and Kyoga Range (in Mbale and Tororo districts). As of July 2006, there were 6 communities with signed CFM Agreements, 5 communities were at different stages of negotiating community forestry agreements with the NFA, with several communities having submitted their applications for consideration. Community Forests presently only exist in

Masindi district. However, with no clear guidelines in place, registration and gazettement of Community Forests overall is yet to be realized.

1.3 Problem Justification

The Ugandan Constitution (1995) provided for the enactment of a Land Act that was to spell out the principles underlying land tenure and management. By recognizing customary tenure, the Land Act (1997) provided communities with a legal framework to organize themselves and develop rules and norms to manage those lands that are common property resources. The Act provides for Communal Land Associations (CLAs) as bodies responsible for the ownership and management of communal land. A CLA can be formed by any group of persons to communally own and manage land on behalf of that group. CLAs may designate all or part of their land for common use. Potential areas CLAs may declare Community Forests (CFs) include natural forests and land to be afforested, as well as areas to be developed as communally-run forest plantations. Thus, CLAs provide a systematic and participatory manner in which community forests can be managed.

In Uganda, the CLA model for the management of community forests has only been piloted in Budongo Sub-county in Masindi District (Western Uganda). Here, a Community-Based Organization, the Budongo Community Development Organization (BUCODO), working with the Forest Sector Co-ordination Secretariat (FSCS) of the then Ministry of Water, Lands and Environment, did pilot Communal Land Associations (CLAs) as institutions through which households and communities could manage community forests

However, despite a wide and growing body of literature on the effectiveness of institutional arrangements at the local level for managing common pool resources (CPRs)[6], there is a dearth of empirical evidence on the effects of the transaction costs resource users face in establishing and sustaining these institutional arrangements on the effectiveness of community forestry initiatives. In the context of community forestry, these costs are incurred in monitoring activities related to institutional design, forest resource use and management, maintenance of the organization and enforcement of property rights to land (forests) and its (their) products.

Although some estimates of transaction costs associated with co-management of fisheries and wildlife exist (Kuperan *et al.* 1998; Mburu, Birner and Zeller 2003); few studies measure the transaction costs of community-based forest management (save for Richards *et al.* 1999; Adhikari and Lovett 2006). Further, economic analysis of participatory forest management has traditionally been biased towards benefits as opposed to costs, especially indirect costs such as transaction costs (Davies & Richards 1999). Thus, while the literature on transaction cost economics offers powerful conceptual insights, these have not been translated into widely accepted operational standards, especially where community forest management is concerned (Benham and Benham 2000).

Equally, while the shifting of central government control over natural resource management to communities is, *a prior,* argued to lead to more efficient management and improvements in the conditions of such resources, a number of studies have highlighted equity and distributional problems, especially the distribution of costs and benefits (Hobley and Wollenberg 1996; Richards *et al.* 1999; Malla 2000; Adhikari, Di Falco and Lovett 2004). However, despite this, the distribution of transaction costs across various sub-groups of resource users is generally not incorporated into an economic analysis of participatory forest management (Davies & Richards 1999; Richards *et al.* 1999). From an institutional economics perspective, this omission leads to failure of communal efforts.

1.4 Objectives of the Study

For households in Budongo Sub-county, where BUCODO did pilot CLA as institutions for managing community forests, this study sought to:

- Examine the level of transaction costs households faced in community forestry and to gauge their effects on community forestry initiatives; and
- Determine the distribution of community forestry transaction costs across households with diverse socio-economic attributes and gauge their effects on community forestry initiatives.

1.5 Research Questions

As a consequence, this study posed the following questions:

1. What level of transaction costs do households face in community forestry and what effect do they have on community forestry initiatives?
2. How significant are transaction costs as a share of total resource benefits and appropriation costs across households with different socio-economic attributes? What does this imply for community forestry initiatives?

1.6 Significance of the Study

By exploring the link between transaction costs in community forestry and their effects on community forestry initiatives, this study should contribute to the growing literature on community forestry and suggest mitigating policy interventions where these costs retard the success of community forestry initiatives. In addition, given the efforts of community-based organizations, donors and government agencies to promote community-based institutional arrangements for the management of communal resources across the developing world, lessons learned should inform policy agendas in countries with similar settings as those presented by Uganda.

1.7 Organization of the Report

Section 2 reviews the extensive literature on community forestry, highlighting the various concepts of community forestry as espoused in sub-Saharan Africa and elsewhere. The role of land tenure regimes on sustainable community forestry, and of institutions and institutional change on transaction costs in natural resource management are also focused upon. The section ends with a review of empirical studies on transaction costs in natural resource management, and as a precursor to the methodology of the study, the theoretical framework that guides the study.

Section 3 presents a description of the general study area, i.e. Budongo sub-county, in whose environs Budongo forest and the communities around the forest reside. The section spells out the specific parishes within the sub-county that were the focus of study and from which data was collected. In addition, methods used to draw the sample, and collect and analyze data are also explained. The section ends with an enumeration of the study's expected results. Section 4 presents and discusses the results of data analysis. Section 5, as last part of the report, presents the conclusion and policy recommendations of the study.

2. CONCEPTS AND CHARACTERIZATION OF COMMUNITY FORESTRY

A number of similar terms are used to describe forestry, which has a community involvement, such as social forestry, community forestry, communal forestry, participatory forestry and joint forest management. Some definitions for these terms are found in *The Dictionary of Forestry* (Helms 1998). Notably, these concepts differ from those describing the [specific] type of forestry, such as agro forestry, farm forestry, non-industrial private forestry, family forestry and urban forestry. In fact, various forms of forestry–with respect to both plantations and native forests – are often involved in a community forestry project.

Five reported definitions of community forestry have been cited by Sarre (1994, 2), who emphasizes participation and benefit sharing and suggests that community forestry be viewed as 'a process of increasing the involvement of and reward for local people, of seeking balance between outside and community interests and of increasing local responsibility for the management of the forest resource'. Sarre's definitions clearly have developing country's situations in mind, as can be inferred from his use of phrases and expressions such as 'a village-level forestry activity … on communal land', 'long-term security of tenure over the forest', and 'people's struggle against domination and exploitation of the community resources by 'outsiders'' (*ibid.*).

It is difficult to trace when and where the current concepts of community forestry first arose. A broad definition was framed by the Food and Agriculture Organization (FAO) as far back as in 1978, that is still being frequently cited:

> Community forestry has been defined ... as any situation, which immediately involves local people in a forestry activity. It embraces a spectrum of situations ranging from woodlots in areas which are short of wood and other forest products for local needs, through the growing of trees at the farm level to provide cash crops and the processing of forest products at the household, artisan or small industry level to generate income, to the activities of forest dwelling communities. It excludes large-scale industrial forestry and any other form of forestry which contributes to community development solely through employment and wages, but it does include activities of forest industry enterprises and public forest services, which encourage and assist forestry activities at the community level. The activities so encompassed are potentially compatible with all types of land ownership. While it thus provides only a partial view of the impact of forestry on rural development, it does embrace most of the ways in which forestry and the goods and services of forestry directly affect the lives of rural people (FAO 1978, 1).

The Regional Community Forestry Training Center for Asia and the Pacific seems to echo this view by defining community forestry as:

> ...... involve(ing) the governance and management of forest resources by communities for commercial and non-commercial purposes, including subsistence, timber production, non-timber forest products, wildlife, conservation of biodiversity and environment, social and religious significance. It also incorporates the practices, art, science, policies, institutions and processes necessary to promote and support all aspects of community based forest management (RECOFTC Strategic Plan 2004, 11).

These definitions clearly identify community forestry in terms of promoting the viability and sustainability of small-scale or non-industrial forestry. In this context, community forestry is perceived as encompassing the distribution of products and services arising from small-scale forestry as well as tree planting activities of communities and individual households. However, regardless of who the community is, based on the above definitions, one can understand that community forestry refers to the promotion of self-reliance, and management and use of trees to improve the livelihoods of community members in a sustainable way.

In this context, community forestry should be understood as a process of increasing the involvement of local people as one dimension of forestry, agriculture, rural energy and other components of rural development. Community forestry is not limited to the management of forests by communities for timber production for sale or household use, but also includes community management for non-timber forest products and non-market forest values, including ecological, cultural, spiritual, recreational and aesthetic values (Colchester *et al.* 2003).

2.1 Approaches to Community Forestry

While differences exist in the operational modalities of community forestry across countries, broad commonalities among processes and paradigms are notable. In the main, these include: commitment of people to the conservation and management of resources; decentralization of power to the locals; the need to achieve the objectives of social, economic and environmental benefits; defined property right; and inclusion of traditional values and ecological knowledge in resource management (Kellert *et al.* 2000).

Differences amongst community forestry modalities are altogether more significant, especially in terms of strategic intentions and approach. One of the most visible is simply where forest local communities are permitted or encouraged to participate in forest management. Management Agreements represent the primary construct of community forestry and enclose whatever arrangement has been reached between community and state. What is actually agreed in the terms of management agreements or contracts varies greatly. With over-simplification, Wily (2003) has drawn the following broad typologies:

- *consultation;*
- *cooperant management where community roles and powers are limited;*
- *contractual partnership* where community roles are more substantial but still inequitable;
- *consigned management* where the community has all operational powers save ultimate authority; and
- *community based forest management,* where jurisdiction is fully devolved, and sometimes including ownership of the estate.

Community forestry initiatives tend to be either mainly product or protection centred in their early focus, and accordingly built mainly around either use (i.e. wildlife (White 1998; Jones 1999; Filimao, Mansur and Namanha 2000); fuel wood extraction (Babin and Bertrand 1998; Ribot 1999); timber harvesting (MINEF 1998); livestock grazing (Kerkhof 2000; Hesse and Trench 2000)) or conservation management issue. Where initiatives are product (use)-centred, local level identification of the community is disposed towards an interest group or user-group focus rather than membership of the community residing within or next to the resource as a whole (Wily 2003). In contrast, community forestry that begins with *protection objectives* tends more strongly towards *management-centred* decision-making and inclusive local groups, irrespective of which members use or do not use the forest. Definition of the community proceeds upon a socio-spatial rather than user basis

The distinctions drawn above reflect the diverse strategic intentions of community forestry. In general, these are either mainly disposed to share forest access or revenue with local populations (*benefit-sharing*) or to share authority over the resource with them (*power-sharing*). As Wily (*ibid.*) points out, the former route seeks less to alter the source of jurisdiction than to obtain local cooperation, while the latter seeks to turn local people into forest managers, either as a matter of right and/or to share the burden of conservation and management with the state. Accordingly, two different paradigms result, as shown in Table 1.

Table 1. Broad distinctions in paradigms

	Benefit Sharing Approaches	**Power Sharing Approaches**
Community as	Beneficiary; User Consultee Rule follower	Actor Manager Decision maker Rule maker Rights centred
Local involvement as	Income centred Use centred Permissive	Management centred Empowerment
Management Objective	To gain cooperation to management	To devolve management
Livelihoods Objective	To share products with communities	To put forest source of livelihood in community hands

SOURCE: Wily (2003)

Classical forms of benefit sharing continue to abound with Buffer Zone developments having the longest history. These are designed to reduce local dependence upon the forest by substitution of especially wood supplies but also sources of livelihood. On-farm tree planting programmes usually feature along with credit opportunities, environmental education programmes[7] and employment opportunities.[8] *Revenue sharing* is another popular means to engage local community support or appease local resentment of the substantial incomes being made in their area by commercial logging, hunting or safari developments. The *legalization of local forest use* is another means towards increasing local collaboration but with associated managerial roles constrained (Vudzijena 1998; Dubois and Lowore 2000; Wild and Mutebi 1996). A more sophisticated approach provides for communities to gain *licensee status*, competing with private sector interests (Ribot 1999; Boyd et al. 2001).

Declared *joint forest management* is widely practised and may embody transfer of a gradually increasing array of decision-making powers to the community level. A greater measure of authority is granted to communities in some countries where the purpose of a *Community Forest* is to demarcate an area where the community may potentially benefit from harvesting but where it also gains managerial control and may determine not to harvest the forest at all (Klein, Salla and Kok 2001; MINEF 1998).

Such initiatives make devolution of controlling jurisdiction their explicit purpose. They do this not only to relocate management as near to the resource as possible, but also to place jurisdiction in the hands of those perceived as having the most lasting vested interest in the forest's survival– for environmental (especially water catchment), socio-ritual and customary reasons, as well as for livelihood benefit. As a matter of course, the approach builds upon local custodial interests, and agreements reached focus upon issues of jurisdiction and sometimes tenure –rather than access. Crucially, the end result is the recognition of the community as owner-manager of the community forest, rather than only a licensee, user or even manager.

2.2 Land Tenure Regimes and Sustainable Community Forestry

Critical to the success of community forestry initiatives are well-defined property rights. Definitions of community forestry remain nebulous, if property rights are not clearly specified, in terms of comprehensiveness, excludability, duration, transferability and benefits conferred. As Treue (2004) points out, the property rights issue is at the core of the emerging themes in contemporary community forestry, including conflict management, political and legal aspects, and economic incentives.

The arguments towards founding community forest management upon secure ownership of the resource are straightforward and succinctly highlighted by Wily (2004). First, lasting local custodianship may logically be expected to be more easily rooted where ownership of the resource is legally clear and secure. That is, as formally acknowledged owners, the community will be able to secure more authority over how the forest is used, regulated and protected. Second, security of tenure logically provides the most profound incentive of all towards sustainable forest conservation, allowing the community to adopt a long-term horizon to management decisions and therefore more cautious conservation measures (FAO 2000; 2003).

Third, once consciously and formally owned by the community, the forest moves from being a relatively open-access resource, to one that gains status as a primary *capital* asset and which, as capital, must be protected to allow a sustainable stream of benefits ('interest') to flow. Fourth, is the impact the recognition of common tenure has on both the rights of the majority and the retention of the area forested. As a formally established, shared community asset, the opportunity arises for majority interests to prevail over those of leaders or economic elites within the community.

2.3 Approaches to Community Forestry in Sub-Saharan Africa

The widening socio-political transformations in the developing world towards more inclusive norms of governance have, in recent years, implied an emergent democratization in the use and management of forest resources. Especially in Africa, early developments in community forestry tended to engage communities as local users whose cooperation was sought and bought by making some of their forest access legal and/or by sharing with them a portion of income generated from forest enterprises.

Thus, Wily (2003) draws broad typologies where *consultation* has epitomized the Forest-Farmer Commissions in Ivory Coast or the Forest Committees in Ghana; *cooperant management* reflecting limited roles and powers for communities epitomizes community forestry in Zimbabwe, Zambia and Benin; *contractual partnership* where community roles are more substantial but still inequitable as in Cameroon, Ethiopia, Nigeria, Madagascar, Sudan, Niger, Mali, Guinea Conakry; *consigned management* where communities have all operational powers save ultimate authority as in The Gambia and Tanzania, and *community based forest management,* where jurisdiction is fully devolved and sometimes includes ownership of the estate as in The Gambia, Malawi, Tanzania, Zanzibar, Lesotho, and potentially Namibia, South Africa and Uganda.

However, forestry administrations have in the recent past come to find that local participation becomes a great deal more meaningful and effective where local populations are involved not as cooperating forest users but as forest managers and/or owners (FAO 2001; 2002). Thus, empowerment of local communities as owner-managers of emergent 'community forests' is gaining particular impetus from corollary land reform strategies that endow customary land interests with much improved status in state law. For example, Uganda's new land law enables customary owners to acquire Certificates of Customary Ownership. In rural Tanzania, an estimated 24 million people may now also acquire a Customary Right of Occupancy, the adjudication and issue of which is made a main purpose of the new Village Land Act 1999. Moreover, in line with customary norms, the law declares that this land right may be held in perpetuity, a right not available to those who have secured their land interests under non-customary regimes and who are limited to 99 year terms.

Whilst provision of new routes for the certification of customary land rights is a clear objective of most of these and similar new laws, registration is in fact of necessity often being made voluntary[9]. This is crucial for the many millions of remote rural occupants who do not currently have the means to have their rights recorded, or who do not see the necessity of this, even where the institutional arrangements have been directly localized to community level, such as in Tanzania, Burkina Faso and Niger. Nevertheless, for countries such as Uganda and Tanzania, land laws limit uncertainty as to the legal effect of failing to register by making it clear that customary rights are held to legally exist irrespective of whether or not they are recorded. This improves the chance for these interests to be upheld in the courts should they face challenges. Also definitions of what is 'customary' are being defined less by tradition than by operating community-supported norms (Wily 2004).

State readiness to empower local people in respect of 'gazetted' or reserved areas is less common with local licensing and revenue sharing tending to still define community forestry. Some countries like Zambia, Cameroon and Burkina Faso restrict local roles to unreserved or other 'poorer' forest areas (*ibid.*). In contrast, community forestry has gained its start in National Forest Reserves in Uganda, Guinea and Ethiopia. Most other states do not proscribe where community forestry may be practiced and developments have begun in both the reserved and unreserved sector but with somewhat different constructs and processes. The question of locus is of course moot in those states where the intention is to transfer nationally owned and administered forests into local hands – most explicitly as is the case in Lesotho, and partially The Gambia, Namibia and South Africa – the latter driven by land restitution policies (Alden and Mbaya 2001).

Furthermore, in Africa there is rarely an in-principle objection to involving communities in the management of commercially important forests, such as industrial plantations. Privatization procedures underway in South Africa have explicitly extended privatization to include communities, not just companies (Mayers, Evans, and Foy 2001). Malawi, Uganda and Tanzania all propose various forms of local participation in future commercial plantation management and one co-management initiative is already underway in Tanzania (*Iddi* 2000).

However, institutional issues increasingly continue to take centre stage where community forestry is concerned and pose the most challenge to the development of effective and democratic norms of local level governance over forests. A main trend is towards defining local community in more inclusive terms and less, in user-centred contexts. The need for stronger and more legal institutional form to entrench local roles is being felt everywhere to enable formal divestment and exercise of meaningful jurisdiction. Issues of accountability are becoming pivotal, both to those with whom management agreements are signed, and internally to make local forest managers accountable to the wider communities upon whose behalf they act.

According to Wily (2003), benefits which go beyond the cost and efficiency benefits of sharing responsibility for forest security and management with citizens that are useful to people, state and forest conservation, may be seen in these paradigm shifts. First, livelihood concerns may be more profoundly and less paternalistically addressed. Generally poor forest-local populations move from positions as subordinate beneficiaries, receiving a share of access, products or other benefits, into positions where they may themselves regulate this source of livelihood and with longer-term perspectives.

An upshot of these developments is that many new forestry laws of necessity now lay out more cautious procedures for declaring or classifying forests (as Government Reserves) and are encouraged to provide alternative routes to securing still unreserved or un-demarcated forests as formally dedicated to the purposes of forest conservation and sustainable use. Community Forests provide this route. Even where Governments remain determined to bring a certain forest under their jurisdiction, consultation with local communities is now widely obligatory as illustrated in most new forest enactments (Textier n.d).

For example, a particularly elaborate and locally accountable procedure for creating new national forest reserves is found in the new Forest Act of Tanzania (2002). The burden is laid upon the state to appoint an investigator to ensure every affected person is properly assisted to make compensation claims. More critical, the investigator is legally bound to investigate whether declaration of a community forest would not be 'a more efficient, effective and equitable route to balance the maintenance of existing rights with the protection and sustainable use of forest resources'[10].

Practical experiences in community forestry confirm this trend. For example, in Tanzania it has been noted that poorer majorities in villages actively use the creation of Village Forest Reserves to prevent not only the capture of commons by the State, but to limit encroachment by powerful groups within the community or outsiders with connections[11]. Also trends towards greater resource ownership and management are premised on the failure of revenue sharing arrangements that sought to co-opt local community support for community forestry (i.e. community forestry initiatives in Zimbabwe, Mozambique, Botswana and Namibia with origins in wildlife-based revenue sharing or in tourism as in Zimbabwe and Kenya).

Conflict over shares has been noted between government and people and within the ranks of the community itself (Negrao 1998). Other difficulties arise where local governments are the conduit for community shares and/or deliver them in the form of social services. Here, supervision costs tend to be high, defeating the need to reduce burdens on the administration

(Mozambique); or service delivery may be 'mired in corruption' as in Cameroon (Fomete 2001), or services provided may be considered locally as irrelevant or the duty of local governments to provide, as in Zimbabwe (Campbell *et al.* 1999). In Ghana, powerful timber interests have been shown to 'delay' arrangements through which they are to directly contribute to the welfare of people within their concession areas (Alden and Hammond 2001).

In conclusion, while there is evidence to suggest that properly defined communal tenure systems serve as a pivotal incentive to effective community based forest management, to work well, communities have to be empowered. Thus, effective community forestry initiatives have to be underpinned by both entrenchment of local tenure *and* jurisdiction. The experience of Mexico with community forestry suggests that while millions of hectares of forests were returned to community ownership in the 1920s, it was only when power to regulate and manage these properties was granted to communities over the last decade, did sustainable and conservationist community based forest management emerge (Bray *et al.* 2003). In this sense, sub-Saharan African countries have some way to go before engendering truly effective community forestry regimes.

2.4 Community Forestry outside Sub-Saharan Africa

The concept of 'social forestry' was first pioneered in India, where it was viewed as a programme of activities designed to assist the rural poor dependent on fuel wood and other forest products (Arnold 1991). However, this social forestry approach collapsed because of the institutional failure of the top-down approach to village use of public forest land (Prasad and Bhatanagar 1995; Ebner 1996; Lawbuary 2004). In its wake, the Joint Forest Management (JFM) model was adopted in the 1980s, which led to great optimism about community empowerment and sustainable forest use (Harrison, Ghose and Herbohn 2001). Unfortunately, Community Forest Management (CFM) in India has often come to be equated with the Joint Forest Management (JFM) movement; something that is opposed by Forestry Department officials who see the term 'community forestry' as entailing strong political connotations of community ownership of forests, which does not exist in India (Apte and Pathak 2002).

The Philippines is recognized as a leader in the development of community forestry programmes. In recent years, community forestry programmes of the Philippines have provided valuable lessons on designing and implementing forestry and other livelihood projects with smallholder communities (Gerrits 1996; Harrison, Emtage, and Nasayao 2004). These programmes are seen to have evolved over time as experience has been garnered on factors leading to success and failure. The multiple objectives of timber production, livelihood for smallholders, sustainable land use and environmental protection are apparent in these programmes. Emtage (2004) has critically reviewed the roles of and challenges faced by the many stakeholder groups involved in community forestry projects in the

Philippine. Challenges to the success of community forestry efforts have been seen to arise from the economically and socially marginalized position of the target communities, the lack of resources available to support the programmes, the lack of physical and social infrastructure in the country, and the continual revision of forestry policies and regulations.

Gregorio, Herbohn, and Harrison (2004) present results of survey research into the role of the forestry nursery sector of Leyte, Philippines, comprising individually owned, communal and government nurseries. Government nurseries appear to have failed to reach the majority of the smallholders, and seedling demand is mostly met by the more numerous and accessible individual and communal nurseries. On the other hand, project initiated communal nurseries are generally not sustainable after the supporting agencies withdraw.

Mangaoang and Cedamon (2004) present a case study of the establishment of a partnership between forestry research institutions (the College of Forestry at Leyte State University) and agro forestry farmers' associations (the Conalum Agroforestry Farmers Association (CAFA)). The strategies adopted to build such partnerships, as well as practical impacts for the community are outlined. The study demonstrates how in-community research can be an effective extension mechanism if community members are given the chance to participate in all of the processes of the research undertaking, commencing at the planning stage, and the research agency has a continuing presence in providing technical support and encouragement.

Estoria, Herbohn, and Harrison (2004) apply a number of indicators to evaluate the performance of community organizers (COs) in Leyte, in their role of facilitating the development, empowerment and sustainable operation of people's organizations (POs) in community forestry. The indicators are based on quantitative and qualitative data obtained from a survey of community organizations and other stakeholders. The study reveals that COs are effective in forming POs, motivating people to participate in voluntary activities, and encouraging cohesiveness among members. However, they point out that the short duration of CO contracts (typically two years) provide insufficient time to establish mature and cohesive POs prepared to assume management on their own, including managing tree plantations. Also, other constraints, including pressure to establish large tree plantations quickly, prevent COs from placing sufficient emphasis on the development and empowerment of the people.

Xu, Zhao, and Suh (2004) review community forestry initiatives in China and describe a community forestry model in Huoshan County. The model has been successful in helping farmers meet the challenge of poverty alleviation through household forestry. Community forestry in China has to some extent replaced the traditional slash-and burn method and the large-scale utilization style of government forestry management. The promotion of independent farmers' organizations is an innovation in modern rural economic cooperation, which has built the capacity of poor farmers in self-development, self-help and self-management, which is necessary for them to escape from the vicious cycle of poverty. As well, it is a way of training those farmers who have skills to take the lead in fighting poverty. Through protection and sustainable utilization of natural resources, community forestry provides village surplus labour and especially women with employment opportunities, and allows farmers to increase their incomes and their ability to pay reasonable agricultural taxes, reducing conflict between the farmers and the government.

Acharya, Petheram, and Reid (2004) note that Nepal places high priority on management of forests for biodiversity, and communities are expected to embrace this requirement. However, there has been little research into community attitudes to biodiversity or even their understanding of the concept. Interviews with individual farmers and focus group discussions in two districts with contrasting geography reveal that the Western term 'biodiversity' is new and confusing to most forest people, who interpret the term in a variety of ways. While there are several related concepts in Nepalese language and rural culture, these are inconsistent among users and therefore of uncertain relevance in designing policy on biodiversity. Harrison, Emtage and Nasayao (2004) suggest the need for some government initiatives to increase awareness about the benefits of high biodiversity in forests. Participatory research, through which scientists and villagers explore existing species diversity and the inclusion of biodiversity conservation measures in community forest operational plans, may help in this regard. .

Malla, Hari and Branney (2003) reported findings of a socio-economic study of Forest User Groups (FUGs) in Nepal, noting the national government policy since the late 1980s of 'transferring the management responsibility for areas of forest (known as community forests) from the Forest Department to FUGs'. Nationally, about 1.4 million rural families have been involved in about 13,000 forest user groups and are managing 1.6 million hectares of forest (Veer 2004). The Federation of Community Forestry Users of Nepal was formed in about 1995 and has a membership of about 5 million farmers, with representation from most of Nepal's 75 districts (FECOFUN 2004).

A number of community forestry initiatives have taken place in Indonesia. The far-reaching decentralization policies in Indonesia have resulted in shifting the forestry focus from national to regional and commune levels. In 1998, the Forestry Department issued a decree recognizing the rights of communities to have permanent control of their forests under community management (World Rainforest Movement 2004). Similarly in Thailand; more than 8,000 separate forests are being managed by local communities (Makarabhirom 2004).

In the USA, the departments of Natural Resources at the state level work to educate citizens and decision-makers about the economic, environmental, psychological and aesthetic benefits of trees and to assist local governments, citizen groups and volunteers in planting and sustaining healthy trees and vegetation wherever people live and work (Washington Department of Natural Resources 2004; Pennsylvania Urban and Community Forestry Council 2004; Alaska Department of Natural Resources 2004). There is a strong emphasis in values of standing trees for local communities[12], with community forestry often viewed as 'urban forestry'. According to this view, a community or urban forest is all the trees growing in and around a city, town, or village. It includes trees in parks, school yards, home landscapes, utility rights-of-way, vacant lots, greenbelts, and along stream banks. Shrubs, ground covers, soil, wildlife, and water bodies are also part of the urban forest. The community forestry model in Canada is similar to that in the USA, but with perhaps a greater emphasis on First Nation communities (Denman Community Forest Cooperative 2004).

In the UK, 'community forestry' takes the form of peri-urban forestry. Here, forests are established in urban fringe areas, to provide well-wooded landscapes 'for work, wildlife, recreation and education' (Roberts and Gautam 2003) and are managed as a partnership between the governmental and non-governmental agencies at the local and national levels (National Community Forest Partnership 2004). Hartebrodt, Fillibrandt, Tand Brandl (2005) note that forests owned by communities – including cities, municipalities, villages and special cooperatives – are one of the main types of forest ownership in Germany.

A key question is what general observations can be drawn about community forestry across these diverse settings with relevance to sub-Saharan Africa. Suffice to say that a major distinction between the community forestry concepts in North America and Europe vis-à-vis those in sub-Saharan Africa is the focus on the various on-site values of trees, as distinct from production of timber and non-wood products for livelihood purposes. Nevertheless, while there would appear to be no single model of community forestry, with arrangements differing between developed and developing countries, and also within each, community forestry programmes do appear to possess a wide variety of characteristics (not all present in any one programme). The characteristics are divided according to institutional and support arrangements, and performance in three sustainability areas, namely economic, social and environmental.

2.5 Theoretical Framework: Prelude to Methodology

2.5.1. *Institutions and Natural Resource Management*

When environmental issues are at stake, analysis often focuses on the way renewable resources are managed or mismanaged by local people. As shown by Adams (1990), the respective discussion centred in the past on the issue of mismanagement and led to approaches of environmental conservation, which were biased in viewing local inhabitants in developing countries as at the core of the problem (Fairhead and Leach 1996). Perhaps one of the most important contributions to this view is the work of Hardin (1968).

Hardin (*ibid.*) draws a link between resource management and institutions by arguing that sustainable resource management is intrinsically linked to regimes of property rights. Hardin attacked *common property regimes* as fraught with free or open access resource use patterns. More problematic for Hardin, was the fact that resource users could not restrain themselves from resource overuse given other resource users' actions (i.e. each seeks to maximize resource extraction) leading to the 'tragedy of the commons'. In a sense, resource users are unable to create rules (institutions) to regulate resource use in a sustainable way.

For Hardin, the only solution was the control of common property resources by a central government or – as suggested by neoclassical economists – the transformation of the commons into private property (Acheson 1989; Feeney *et al.* 1990). The tragedy bias led many governments to take the resource rights and responsibilities out of the hands of local groups and to legitimize this by pointing out that existing overuse of forests, wildlife, fisheries and pastures were the result of this tragedy. Hardin was later criticized for misinterpreting common property as an open access, given the fact that resources which in many cases appear open access are indeed owned by local groups, village groups, and lineage or kinship groups (Acheson 1989). With these resources access is only open to members of a particular group and strangers [are] authorized to access the resource by the resource owning group.

Anthropological research also shows that inside such a group of users there are mostly rules and norms regulating the amount of off-take of such a resource (time scales, quotas, technical regulations, etc.). Additionally, there are monitoring and sanctioning boards (council of elders, priests, young men, i.e. warrior age classes). As well, the close face-to-face interaction in a small-scale society, where social control is everywhere, can be regarded as working as a monitoring and sanctioning device. In short, communities' local resource use patterns are governed by *institutions* (regulative devices), which define who is allowed to use what kind of resource, at what time and under what conditions.

The way how such institutions evolve and change and what influence they have on the economic strategies of individuals and groups of actors, are issues debated by different theories in economic history, political science and anthropology. Different approaches can be subsumed under the label of New Institutionalism (North 1990; Ostrom 1990; Ensminger 1992; 1998; Broomley 1992; Becker & Ostrom 1994; Ruttan 1998; Gibson 1999). Institutions are seen here as formal and informal "rules of the game", such as constraints, norms, values and rules. These give incentives to groups and individuals, and also structure human action and interaction, especially in economic activities, in collective action and in sustainable resource use. They help individuals form expectations about the others' conduct, thereby enabling co-ordination and cooperation. Institutions, such as property rights systems or laws, are developed by the state (formal institutions) or by local communities, where they are embedded in their culture (informal institutions).

An important aspect of explaining how institutions operate is illustrated by the work of North (1990). He not only states that institutions matter for economic activities, but that if institutions work properly they reduce *transaction costs*. In the case of the management of common property resources (CPR), Ruttan (1998) shows another interesting aspect by focusing on the gains enabled by co-operative institutions.[13] Nevertheless, the assertion that institutions are always optimal is ludicrous when confronted with reality. Institutions created by man are not always optimal, efficient and egalitarian. Thus, without careful empirical analysis (which is rare) functionalist explanations may become justifications for irrational or non-functional institutions.

There seems no reason to suppose *a priori* that competitive pressures are always sufficient to break up less than optimal institutions. Institutions do not always decrease transactions costs but might actually, when they are inefficient, increase transaction costs (Olsson 1999). Based on review study on CPR management in Zimbabwe, Campbell *et al.* (2001) argue that there is a fair degree of misplaced optimism about CPR institutions since the formal rule-based system that form the cornerstones of CPR management are gradually replaced by donor-assisted interventions rooted in norm-based controls.

North (1990) has pointed out that not all institutions are efficient and powerful groups to serve their particular interests can capture institutions of collective action. In addition, it may be the richer members of the community that dominate local politics and organizations (Saxena 1989). Thus, understanding the determinants and impact of common property institutions and distributional implications of CPR regime is essential for informing forest policies and programmes in developing countries where much policy emphasis currently is being placed on promoting community-based institutions for forest resource management and poverty reduction.

Two forms are principally responsible for the development of such co-operative rules, as seen in CPR-institutions. CPR-institutions can develop under the rule of reciprocity ("reciprocal altruism") or under a form of asymmetrical power relations ("asymmetric reciprocity" or "clientilism"). In "reciprocal altruism" the different actors can profit from co-operation, for example, if they allow access of foreign users to the resource, because in a later time they may be able to profit from the resources of those foreign users. With "asymmetrical altruism", co-operation in an unbalanced situation of power relation is understood. In this situation, there may be cooperation from the side with lesser power, even when he or she enjoys taking lesser profits than the stronger side, because this profit is still greater than if he or she would not co-operate at all.

In the debate on common property and sustainability, the notion of Hardin's "Tragedy of the Commons" paradigm can actually be undermined by taking a close look at how CPR-institutions are operating. Ostrom's (1990) work illustrates this by analyzing different CPR institutions and their management by local communities all over the world. By looking at successfully operating, locally developed CPR-institutions, Ostrom highlights eight *design principles* (DPs) as depicted in Table 2, which can actually be included in the notion of transaction costs; i.e. if CPR-institutions are to operate properly, they in fact must reduce these costs.

Table 2. Design principles (DPs) for effective institutions for sustainable natural resource use

Clearly Defined Boundaries
The boundaries of resource systems (e.g. groundwater basin or forest) and the individuals or households with rights to harvest resource products are clearly defined.

Proportional Equivalence Between Benefits and Costs
Rules specifying the amount of resource products that a user is allocated are related to local conditions and to rules requiring labour, materials and/or money inputs.

Collective-Choice Arrangements
Most individuals affected by harvesting and protection rules are included in the group who can modify these rules.

Monitoring
Monitors, who actively audit physical conditions and user behaviour, are at least partially accountable to the users and/or are users themselves.

Graduated Sanctions
Users who violate rules are likely to receive graduated sanctions (depending on the seriousness and context of the offence) from the users, from officials accountable to these users, or from both.

Conflict-Resolution Mechanisms
Users and their officials have rapid access to low-cost, local arenas to resolve conflict among users or between users and officials.

Minimal Recognition of Rights to Organize
The rights of users to devise their own institutions are not challenged by external governmental authorities, and users have a long-term tenure rights to the resource.

Nested Enterprises (For resources that are part of larger systems)
Appropriation, provision, monitoring, enforcement, conflict resolution, and governance activities are organized in multiple layers of nested enterprises.

SOURCE: Becker and Ostrom 1995:119, (in Ostrom 1990:56f.)

Ostrom (1990) clearly shows that the DPs are not universal rules, which guarantee success in all situations. Moreover, these are principles to be adapted to local conditions. Becker and Ostrom (1995) argue that institutional diversity found among local communities is often better adapted to the variability and insecurities in chaotic ecosystems (e.g. change in fish stock population) than strategies based on biological-mathematical models.[14] Additionally, two of the eight aspects (regarded as important for the building up of new institutions) are particularly relevant in raising the questions of whether: actors involved have common or different interests (i.e. homogeneity or heterogeneity of interests) or value the future in respect to the use of the resource in question.

Economic heterogeneity and high rates of discounting the future make it very difficult to establish long-term CPR institutions for sustainable resource use, as it is much more difficult to act collectively and to develop rules in situations where everyone follows their own interests. Additionally, when there are high rates of discounting the future, rational resource users seek to use up the resource as fast as possible, because what remains is immediately taken by others. In this situation, the value of keeping resources for later use is close to zero. These are two aspects which lead to an overuse of renewable resources (Becker and Ostrom 1995).

Some economic and social science literatures emphasize that homogeneity or heterogeneity among agents in any society reflects the levels of trust, which influences the emergence of local management institutions through its impact on costs of transactions. Transaction costs associated with trading are reduced by an increase in levels of trust between trading partners and the development of institutions that provide incentives for lasting cooperation (North 1990; Ostrom 1994). Zak and Knack (2001) posit that heterogeneous societies, especially those with weak formal and informal institutions, have lower trust and retarded economic performance than less heterogeneous, higher trust societies.

Nonetheless, in many empirical studies, physical input and property rights are taken as variables and transaction costs of resource management, seldom incorporated in the 'price' of resource consumption, though they can be a significant component of resource use. It has been reported that transaction costs of community-based forest management are significantly higher for poorer users (Richards *et al.* 1999). In many cases, benefits from resource management are exceeded by management costs (Hanna 1995).

A common property regime would not have the need for extensive records on boundaries and sales, but instead require meetings and discussions where the co-owners decided their strategies for the coming period, which constitute a significant portion of management costs (Bromley 1991). Most of the recent literature on heterogeneity and collective action presume that socio-economic differentiation and group heterogeneity makes cooperative arrangements more difficult and innovation of local management institutions becomes impossible due to high transaction cost.

There has been some critiques of this approach centering especially on the *methodological individualism*, its formalistic aspect and its blindness to historical and social context. This critique comes from scientists dealing with evolutionary economics and development studies discussing problems of participation as the "New Tyranny" (Cleaver 2001). Cleaver (*ibid.*) points out that the rational choice theorem of methodological individualism is not suited for an analysis that shall help to solve problems faced with participation in development.

This point seems unjustified as Cleaver's work and indeed the well addressed critique on participatory approaches show: The critical factor in development projects is the incentive (be this economic, political, social, psychological or so called "cultural") an individual has in reference to his/her position in the community or society. To study this carefully is one of the aims of the New Institutionalism. Secondly, it is difficult to grasp Cleaver's critique of Ostrom's approach to institutions. As Cleaver understands it, Ostrom opts for a formalization of institutions, which can have negative effects, for example, by excluding those who are financially or from the working force of their household not able to participate in a development project. Additionally it is criticized that only formal institutions (by the state or by a development corporation) is the solution to the problem.

However, Ostrom does only draw lessons from successful cases all over the world, which not all rely exclusively on "formal" institutions. On the contrary, she stresses that so-called informal institutions embedded in a specific culture are as successful as formal ones or even more successful. Additionally she opts for the recognition of the local and indigenous knowledge of resource flows. Where Cleaver is right, is the fact that regarding the first principle – clear boundaries – these sometimes cannot be as clearly defined as Ostrom's work suggests, especially when considering changes in resource flows from one season to another. Additionally, it is clear that to distinguish between "formal" and "informal" institutions is a delicate thing; traditional (and some would say informal) institutions can be as formalized or even more formalized than the institutions built up by the state.

2.5.2. Transaction Costs in Natural Resource Management

Transaction costs have become an important topic in environmental and natural resource policy in recent years; with the concept being incorporated by various scholars (see Coase 1960; Cheung 1983; Alchian & Demsetz 1972; North 1990) into the school of institutional economics. This school argues that only those societies that succeed in creating institutions[15] that effectively reduce transaction costs will endure (North 1990).

Transaction costs refer to those costs that arise when individuals exchange ownership rights to economic assets and enforce their exclusive rights. Holloway *et al.* (2000) define transaction costs as "the costs of searching for a partner (or group) with whom to exchange, screening potential partners to ascertain their trustworthiness, bargaining with potential partners (and officials) to reach an agreement, transferring the products, monitoring the agreement to see that its conditions are fulfilled, and enforcing the exchange agreement".

In the context of community-based resource management, these costs are incurred in the form of negotiation, monitoring of activities related to institutional design, maintenance of the organization and enforcement of property rights to land and its products. Where, as in many developing countries; institutional changes in resource management have shifted from central government control to community-based management, transaction costs economics has come to be considered a potential tool for development policy analysis and in particular, the assessment of the effectiveness of institutional arrangements in resource management (Mburu, Birner, and Zeller 2003).

However, measurement of transaction costs can be problematic. Benham & Benham (2000) point out four factors that make empirical measurement of transaction costs difficult. These include: lack of a clear-cut definition of transaction costs; difficulties in separating transaction costs from production costs as they are often jointly determined; many forms of transactions may not take place when the cost of transacting is very high; and many estimates may be required as individuals and groups in any given society face various opportunities and thus transaction costs.

In understanding why any particular transaction is likely to be adopted by an individual, knowledge of the opportunity costs faced by that individual is required (*ibid.*). Hanna (1995) has observed that in many field settings, efficient management of common pool resources is often challenged by the various sources of uncertainty, which result in high transaction costs. Production costs have also been shown to be another category of cost in community-based resource management, incurred because of the opportunity cost of land set aside for community forests as well as establishing infrastructure to manage the resources (Mburu, Birner, and Zeller 2003).

As many forest products are public environmental goods and services (with non-rivalry in consumption and difficulty in exclusion), high transaction costs are incurred in delineating property rights and preventing free-riding. Transaction cost economics literature describes four key attributes of transactions relevant to natural resource management (Williamson 1991;

Fenoaltea 1984; Birner and Wittmer 2000): uncertainty, asset specificity, frequency and care or effort intensity.

Hanna (1995) describes four different resource management stages in which variable transaction costs are inevitable: the description of the resource context, regulatory design, implementation, and enforcement of agreed upon rules. Thus, efficient management of common property resources is often challenged by sources of uncertainty that result in high levels of transactions costs. Asset-specificity can be defined as investment in assets specifically relevant for a particular transaction that generates quasi rents. Most of the physical assets in the form of natural resources (forests, wildlife, fish, etc.) are very site specific. Frequency of decision-making is another attribute of transaction as many activities carried out to implement management decisions are frequent, ranging from daily to seasonal (Birner and Wittmer 2000). While effort-intensive transactions are related to production activities, care-intensive transactions are characteristic of protection activities (Fenoaltea 1984).

At the community level, transaction costs of collective action are influenced by the physical characteristics of a resource and social capital of the community members (Ostrom 1994; Baland and Platteau 1996) since these factors influence the achievement of certain outcomes that would not be attainable otherwise (Coleman 1990; Molians 1998). Since local resource users usually get degraded types of forests at hand-over of government forests to a community, considerable start-up costs are incurred to make the system economically viable. It may happen that benefits generated by collective action are exceeded by management costs (Hanna 1995).

Transaction costs may differ across households because of household characteristics and incentives as well as disincentives created by management institutions. Socio-economic status, gender, and ethnicity of individual community members may limit the opportunity to participate in the decision-making activities that determine extent of transaction costs. Zak and Knack (2001) emphasize that homogeneity or heterogeneity among agents in any society reflects the level of trust, which influences the emergence of local management institutions through their impact on costs of transactions. All these issues inform the methodology adopted in this study.

2.5.3 Empirical Studies on Transaction Costs in Natural Resource Management

Although transaction cost economics provides a useful tool to understand the functioning of community-based management system, it has been applied in a limited number of forestry studies (Leffler and Rucker 1991; Wang and van Kooten 1999; Zhang 2000; 2001; Adhikari and Lovett

2006). A few empirical studies attempt to measure transaction costs in other forms of natural resource management regimes. For example, Crocker (1971) conducted an empirical analysis of the role of transaction costs in natural resource transfer using the case of the impact of air pollution on agricultural land use. He concluded that the transaction costs of affected farmland owners bargaining with polluters were very high.

Leffler and Rucker (1991) applied transaction cost analysis to the structure of timber harvesting contracts and established empirical evidence for the influence of specific types of transactions costs on contractual provisions. In order to quantify the transaction costs of fisheries co-management, Kuperan *et al.* (1998) undertook a study on San Salvador Island in the Philippines. They argue that monitoring emerges as the activity accounting for more than 50 per cent of the total costs of all the activities involved in co-management. It takes up the bulk of the time as it is a continuous day-to-day activity and is crucial for institutional maintenance.

Aggarwal (2000) undertook a case study of group-owned wells in Southern India in an attempt to understand the possibilities and limitations to cooperation in small groups by looking at the transaction costs associated with these activities. She observed that costs of negotiating were likely to be higher in the case of well expansion activities, particularly in groups where heterogeneity among members in terms of their endowments and needs is high.

In developed countries, Kumm and Drake (1998) estimated the private transaction costs incurred in relation to participation in a Swedish agri-environmental programme with data collected from a survey of 90 randomly selected farmers. They found that transaction costs as a share of actual compensation received were typically around 12 per cent and private transaction costs have risen over recent years. Falconer (2000) also observed a significant level of transaction costs associated with participation in European agri-environment programmes, and argued that if such costs are not taken into account in policy evaluation, there is a risk of sub-optimal policy prescription.

3. METHODOLOGY

3.1 General Study Area

This study was undertaken in Budongo sub-County in Masindi District (Western Uganda) along the fringes of Budongo Forest. Budongo Forest covers an area of 793 km², of which only 53 per cent is forest. The remaining 47 per cent is grassland. The altitudinal range is 700-1270m. This forest type is classified as medium altitude semi-deciduous moist forest. Budongo has a high biodiversity with 24 species of small mammals, nine being primates; 465 species of trees and shrubs; 359 species of birds; 289 species of butterflies; and 130 species of moths (Forest Department 1996). Budongo Forest Reserve was gazetted in 1932. Commercial extraction of timber has been ongoing since 1915. Today, some 77 per cent of this forest has been cut at least once. The report by Forest Department (1996), states that Budongo is in a serious 'state of degradation' due to the high levels of illegal pit sawing, hunting and human encroachment.

From 2001 to 2004, an evaluation of prospects for using indigenous trees for Agroforestry in an external buffer zone around Uganda's Budongo Forest was undertaken. The six parishes of Biiso, Kabango, Kibwona, Kasenene, Nyanttozi and Nyabyeya in Budongo sub-county were included. The evaluation involved dialogue with Budongo Forest buffer zone residents and assessing tree populations in the forest. The dialogue ascertained how trees are incorporated into farm activities, their importance to local people for products, and how people ranked alternative species available. Assessment of tree population status of extensively used species by forest sectors adjacent to the parishes was undertaken.

It is within these parishes that the Forestry Inspection Division (FID) and a community-based organization, the Budongo Community Development Organization (BUCODO), did pilot the management of community forests using Communal Land Associations (CLAs). BUCODO is an indigenous voluntary CBO initiated by the local communities living around the Budongo Forest Reserve in 1998. Its vision is stated as the creation of a

> ...forest community free from exploitation, injustice, environmental degradation and pollution, having a scope for self reliance and to develop a relation of universal brotherhood irrespective of economic status, political, gender, religious and educational differences.

To this end, BUCODO seeks to improve the livelihoods and welfare of the local communities by conserving the environment through development. BUCODO focuses its interventions in areas of:

- Population (reproductive health, youth development and child rights) and natural resource management (promoting best conservation practices for the sustainable use of natural resources e.g. CFM, Agro-Forestry, Community Forests Management, Energy Saving Technology);
- Poverty alleviation (promoting alternative and sustainable forest based/friendly income generating activities); and
- Capacity building (of organisations and partners in order to realize sustainable development).

3.2 Specific Study Sites

There are 60 identified pilot community forests in Budongo, of which only three have been well-developed in the pilot. The community forests in the parishes of Kabango, Nyanttozi and Nyabyeya constituted the study sites for this project. These parishes have a multi-ethnic population composed of the indigenous Banyoro and migrants including the Alur, Kebu, Lugbara, Madi, Lendu and Bagungu. In addition, over the last 20 or so years, these parishes have seen an influx of internally displaced persons (IDPs), who, on account of the war situation in some districts in northern Uganda, have moved in to these areas.

The study communities are surrounded by tropical hardwood forests. The major local uses of the forests are for fuel wood and water collection. Building materials from poles and logs are also significant in the local economy. However, timber harvesting is generally not part of local economic activities. Auxiliary uses include medicinal and food plants, as well as other forest products. These communities are made up mostly of sedentary arable farmers. The main food crop is maize, whereas the key cash crop is tobacco. Most land holdings are customary with households possessing, on average, two acres.

3.3 Community Forestry in the Study Sites

In the study areas, Collaborative Forest Management (CFM) initiatives should be understood as local residents' use and management of community forests under yet unregistered CLAs on the fringes of the main Budongo forest. Nevertheless, in these areas many of these so called *community forests* have been unsustainably harvested of timber. The illegal felling of timber, charcoal burning and crop farming within the community forests highlights how dependent some community members are on these community forests. It is in this light that BUCODO compliments its community forestry initiatives with a number of other community development projects, which seek to lessen households' dependence on community forests.

For example, BUCODO's Integrated Conservation and Reproductive Health Project (BICHRP) seeks to secure the conservation and regeneration of community forests by enabling community members to realise reproductive health, resource conservation measures and income generating activities in an integrated, gender-sensitive and sustainable manner. Through the project, reproductive health services are made available, resource conservation best practices are adopted, and communities are mobilized and sensitized for community forestry.

While conservation practices are heavily promoted by BUCODO, promoted too is the sustainable harvesting of key forest products for market. Thus, BUCODO has implemented other projects which aim at commercialising resource harvesting activities in community forests. The Community Based Commercial Cultivation of Medicinal Plants (BUCCOMA) project seeks to promote the production and trade of medicinal plants as an alternative income-generating activity and to reduce the illegal felling of timber. Activities such as the production and marketing of *Occimum Kilimandscharicum*-based Nuturub Ointment at a factory in Nyabyeya parish, energy saving technologies, conservation education and enhancement of capacity in management, entrepreneurship and technical skills have also been successfully implemented under this project.

The National Forest Authority, being the government 'responsible body' with whom CLAs partner, has offices in Nyabyeya parish and provides guidelines on how forest resources in the Central Forest Reserves can be accessed and harvested. These include advices on the harvest of timber (which requires the acquisition of licence), the designation of charcoal burning zones, and the demarcation of buffer zones for resource harvest, beyond which encroachments into the main Budongo forest is prohibited. In addition, the NFA employs guards who patrol the forest to enforce these guidelines.

In a nutshell, Collaborative Forestry Management in the study areas constitutes a multitude of interventions aimed at promoting the sustainable use and management of community forests under the auspices of community members, BUCODO and the NFA. The contents of these interventions are diverse and include practices to promote resource use and management, best practices, and broad initiatives in support of community development.

3.4 Methods, Data Collection and Analysis

Primary data on household level variables and the use and management of community forests was collected through a questionnaire administered to household heads and/or other competent household members in the three parishes of Kabango, Nyabyeya and Nyantonzi. A stratified random sample of households was drawn from a census list of village households. This sampling method sought to categorise all households into three ranks, i.e. poor, middle wealth and rich, based on land holding size. Poor households were taken to own between 0 to 1 acre of land, middle-wealth households to own between 1 and 5 acres, and rich households to own over 5 acres of land. In total, 258 households were sampled across the sub-county (see Table 3).

Table 3. Distribution of sample households, by parish and land holding size

Parish	Socio-economic status (size of Land holding)			Total
	Poor	Middle wealth	Rich	
	(Land <1	1 acres< Land <	Land>5acres	

		acre)	5 acres		
Kabango	Count	12	34	13	59
	(%) in parish	20.3%	57.6%	22.0%	100.0%
Nyabyeya	Count	25	51	29	105
	(%) in parish	23.8%	48.6%	27.6%	100.0%
Nyantonzi	Count	17	40	37	94
	(%) in parish	18.1%	42.6%	39.4%	100.0%
Total	Count	54	125	79	258
	(%)Total sample	20.9%	48.4%	30.6%	100.0%

While land size holding formed the basis upon which the sample was drawn, it was felt that this categorization was a limiting factor in assessing the socio-economic position of what appeared to be equally positioned households (at least from an economic point of view). Thus, in much of the subsequent analysis, relations between key household variables of interest (e.g. participation in community forestry, levels of transaction costs incurred in community forestry, etc) were tested against land holding size and other household socio-economic indicators, such as household value holdings of tools (farm implements), livestock and total household assets (i.e. the total value of tools, livestock and other household use and consumer assets).

The household questionnaire, which was administered by the principal researcher and three research assistants, was designed to collect data on households' use and management of community forests in order to allow the computation of community forestry transaction costs, and consequently, to examine their effects on community. To this end as well, other household information, such as bio-data, ownership of assets, household farm and non-farm activities undertaken, household level of awareness and participation in community forestry, etc., was collected in order to further explore links between a household's socio-economic position and its participation in community forestry. [16]

Questions on transaction costs mainly focused on teasing out respondents' responses on time they or household members spent participating in various community forestry activities, with a direct bearing on the enforcement of community-based property rights over the forests, e.g. attending village forestry meetings, monitoring others' forest resource use and management practices, and attending meetings to sanction or resolve conflicts around the use and management of community forests. Data was also collected on the amount of time household members spent in collecting, processing and transporting a unit of forest products from community forest to house, rural hourly wages in agriculture, the costs and economic life of farm implements, etc.[17]. Based on these data, it was possible to estimate resource appropriating costs, transaction costs and value of benefits households derived from the use and management of their community forests. Using costs and benefits thus obtained, net benefits for households defined across various socio-economic rankings were calculated.

Open-ended discussion with groups of forest users, the NFA and BUCODO officials provided additional information. This was instrumental in triangulating some of the information provided by the households on for example, forest user's patterns of resource extraction and maintenance, village level decision-making processes for community forestry, the nature of transaction costs faced in community forestry, and institutional and legal constraints. A number of data analysis methods were employed to tease out a host of relationships using bivariate analysis methods. The statistical programme SPSS was employed to cross tabulate and find significance between the various variables of interest in order to meet the study's objectives and answer the key research questions.

3.5 Expected Results

This study was expected to have the following results:

1. Contribute to and broaden existing literature on common pool resource management by incorporating transaction costs into the economic analysis of community forestry;

2. Showing that transaction costs in community forestry entail adverse effects for the success of community forestry initiatives -effects which in turn may be variably distributed across socio-economically differentiated households; the study's findings should enrich policy debates and decision on how best to mitigate the adverse effects of transaction costs on community forestry efforts;

3. Disseminate the study's findings through a workshop to be attended by a host of forestry sector stakeholders including Community Based Organizations, governmental agencies/officials (national and local government), group of and/or individual forest users, etc; and

4. To publish the study's findings in economic journals that focus on environment and resource management issues.

4. STUDY RESULTS

4.1 Survey Population

The survey collected information on 258 households. These domestic units count a total of 1519 persons between them, with an average of 5.9 persons per households, which was slightly higher than the national average of 5.2 given by the UNHS 2005/06.[18] Respondents' gender was unevenly distributed in the sample, with males and females constituting respectively 81 and 19 per cent of respondents. The civil status of household heads/respondents was significantly associated with their gender. Thus, over 95 per cent of male heads live with their spouse, whereas only 40 per cent of female heads do. Sixty per cent of female-heads in the sample were widowed. On the other hand, male household heads rarely lived without a spouse; being single, widowed or other (probably divorced or separated) in only about 4 per cent of cases (see Table 4).

Table 4. Key household-level statistics

Gender characteristics of sample households (per cent of sample)		
	Male	Female
Proportion of Respondents	81%	19%
Respondent Household Status*		
Household Head	97.6	2.4
Others	15.4	84.6
Household attributes by type of household (per cent)		
Civil status	Male headed	Female-headed
Married	95.5%	40%
Single	3.5%	
Widowed	0.5%	60%
Other	0.5%	
Mean age of HH head	39.08	35.53
Mean number of HH members	6.0	5.6

Female household heads were also likely to be younger than their male counterparts, which may be explained by the fact that these women become heads when widowed at an early age. The mean number of persons living in female headed households is also lower than that in male headed units; further validating the observation that early widowhood (on account of war, HIV/AIDS etc.) may have denied women heads of households the opportunity to have as many children as their counterparts in male-headed households.

The majority of respondents, about 63 per cent, claimed to have been born in the localities where they presently resided, while close to over to 30 per cent claimed to have resided in their present localities for over 5 years. Only about 7 per cent of respondents claimed to have resided in their present communities for less than 5 years (Table 5). All respondents also claimed to belong to some religious affiliation; with the majority claiming to be Christians[19] (i.e. 96.1 per cent), and a small minority claiming to be Muslims (i.e. 3.9 per cent). As pertains to the ethnic milieu in the study communities, close to half of all respondents were Lugbara, who, surprisingly are not indigenous to the study areas. The indigenous Banyoro and Alur constituted only 32 per cent of respondents. Other tribes constituted the remaining 19 or so per cent of respondents.

Table 5. Years in residence categories

Years of residence in locality	Frequency	Per cent
1 – 2 years	8	3.1
3 – 5 years	9	3.5
5 or more years	79	30.6
Born in locality	162	62.8
Total	258	100.0

No statistically significant relation was found linking ethnicity and respondents' length of years in residence in the study areas[20] which, together with the fact that the majority of respondents belonged to non-indigenous groups, validated the view that most were long-standing migrants. This finding has implications for the state of social capital at the community level, which for diverse peoples as those sampled can be expected to be low and to raise transaction costs in community forestry.

The role insecurity in the war ravaged parts of northern and western Uganda has played in drawing influxes of Internally Displaced Persons (IDPs) to the study areas, beyond putting great pressure on community forest resources has also stifled and raised transaction costs in community Forestry. Respondents cited instances where gaining community members' effective cooperation in community forestry was difficult in situations where IDPs were likely to engage in opportunistic behaviour with respect to community forestry activities because they did not view their stay in the study areas as longstanding. The influx of non-indigenous groups of people in the study areas also means that the authority of traditional leaders to mobilize communities for collective action has been compromised which, together with the role local politicians play in legitimizing the forest encroachment practices of landless migrants and IDPs, has undermined community forestry initiatives.

With regard to levels of education, the majority (56.6 per cent) of respondents had some basic (primary) education; 22.1 per cent had some secondary education, while 1.2 per cent per cent had some post-secondary and university education. However, a substantial proportion (20.2 per cent) of respondents claimed to have no formal education of any kind.

4.2 Household Asset Ownership

Over 48 per cent of households in the sample had at their disposal land holdings averaging 1 to 5 acres. No gender disparities appeared to exist with respect to land size holdings, although men household heads appeared disadvantaged at the lower end of the land size holding continuum. Thus, 22 per cent of male household heads owned land of 1 or less acres compared to 16.3 per cent for female household heads. While this finding appears interesting (i.e. that men might be more disproportionately represented among the poor on the land size holding measure), the fact that male respondents were disproportionately represented in the sample means the result has to be viewed with some scepticism.

In terms of a relation between land size holdings and the land tenure regime, more (38.9 per cent) of the households with land sizes of 1 acre or less, had customary tenure rights. A substantial proportion (35.2 per cent) of these households also appeared landless, being able to access land through land rental markets or by obtaining land leases; 14.8 per cent were squatters while 11.1 per cent claimed to have freehold ownership over their land. For those households holding land in excess of 1 acre, the majority held it in the form of customary rights. Significant minorities also held it in the form of freeholds, with leases also featuring prominently within these land size categories. Squatting households and those renting land were less important in those land size holding categories in excess of 1 acre.

With regard to the holding of livestock, only 2.3 per cent of households claimed to own cattle. Poultry, goats and pigs were the key commonly held livestock types. However, on average very few units across all livestock types were held by households. Average total household wealth held in livestock was only Uganda shillings 86,528 (US$ 53.41)[21].

While in their majorities households appeared to possess most critical farm implements necessary to work their lands, equally evident was the small numbers of such implements held; suggesting an inefficient household use of these implements given average household sizes of about 5.9 persons. Hoes, machetes, axes and jerry cans (used to collect water) appeared to be the key farm implements held by the majority of households. On average, households held Ugandan shillings 48,529 (US $30) in farm implements.

Data was also collected on the ownership of various household use and consumer-oriented assets, such as beds, tables, chairs, radios, bicycles, motorbikes, mobile phones, TVs, refrigerators and cars/trucks. It goes without saying that, save for the first four items and mobile phones, almost all households were asset-poor with respect to the other items.

Nevertheless, for those households that owned some of these items, their value constituted a substantial measure of household wealth. Thus, on average households held Ugandan shillings 238,350 (US$ 147) in household use and consumer related assets.

4.3 Households' Farm Activities

All households diversified their productive activities and reported undertaking a combination of crop farming, livestock rearing and forestry activities. Close to 43 per cent of households cited maize as the most important food crop item grown, with cassava coming second at close to 40 per cent of households. Other crops were most important for the remaining households and included sweet potatoes (5.8 per cent), millet (8.2 per cent) and other crops (3 per cent). As regards to the marketing of food crops, close to 46 per cent of households cited maize to be their key marketable food crop, followed by cassava, 38 per cent of households. Thus, in the study communities, maize and cassava appeared to play an important role as both food and cash crops. Poultry was the main livestock type reared by households (i.e. 52.3 per cent of the households), followed by goats (35.7 per cent). A few households also kept other forms of livestock: pigs (7 households), sheep (1 household), and cattle (1 household)]. Nineteen (7.4 per cent) households kept no livestock of any kind. The majority (52 per cent) of households cited poultry to be the main type of livestock they marketed. The marketing of goats was also important for 35 per cent of the households.

4.4 Household Non-Farm Activities

One hundred and twenty-one or 46.9 per cent of households claimed to engage in a number of non-farm activities to diversity and supplement farm income. Table 6 gives a breakdown of the types of non-farm activities households undertook. Thus, over half of the households who undertook non-farm activities were engaged in some forms of commercial activity (i.e. trading/shop keeping). A significant percentage (15 per cent) of households also diversified into non-farm activities such as craftwork, brick making, the dispensing of herbal medicines and brewing. Brick making was a particularly important non-farm activity, being undertaken by household members of at least 14.9 per cent of households who had members engaged in non-farm activities. Craftwork, brewing and the dispensing of traditional medicines were less important for most households undertaking non-farm activities.

Table 6. Numbers and per cent of households undertaking various non-farm activities

Non-farm activities	Number	per cent
Trading	32	26.4
Shop-keeping	29	24.8
Cottage industry-crafts	8	6.6
Traditional herbalists	6	5.0
Bricks making	18	14.9
Brewing	9	7.4
Any combination of non-farm activities	18	14.9
Total	120	100.0

On hundred and eighteen (45.9 per cent) of households reported that at least one household member was engaged in sales of labour services as reported in Table 7. Thus, 35.6 per cent of these households had a member engaged in agricultural labour sales within the community, 31.4 per cent in non-agricultural labour sales within the community, and 2.5 per cent engaged in labour sales outside the community (i.e. outside Budongo sub-county). 29.7 per cent of these households had members who sold labour through a combination of the preceding three modes.

Table 7. Numbers and per cent of households undertaking labour sales

Off-farm activities	Number	per cent
Agricultural-labour sales in community	42	35.6
Non agricultural-labour sales in community	37	31.4
Labour sales outside Budongo sub-county	3	2.5
Any combination of off-farm activities	36	29.7
Total	118	100.0

A statistically significant relationship (Chi square =42. 237 p< 0.000) also existed between those households with members engaged in non-farm and sales of labour activities, which suggested that households that diversified outside agriculture were more likely to have members engage in both labour sales and commercial activities of varying types. Also, the question of whether households had members who diversified their economic activities this way was strongly related to key household economic variables (i.e. values of household's productive and livestock assets, and land size holding), suggesting that diversification was overall more important for those households who were most marginal from an assets point of view (see Appendix 5).

4.5 Household Asset Position, Economic Activities and Community Forestry

The fact that land poor households were also more likely to access land through rental markets and squatting provides additional evidence of their need to encroach on community forests. Also, it was these households who, more than their richer neighbours, showed greater frequency in visiting community forests to procure edible plants. Equally significant was the finding that non-farm and off-farm economic activities were overall more important for those households who were most marginal from an assets point of view. The implication of these findings is that for marginal households, incentives exist to engage in suboptimal resource use and management practices either because these households were assets poor or lacked opportunities for household members to find non-farm work.

4.6 Household Use of Community Forests

Across the sample, firewood and water were the key forest products households procured from community forests. A substantial proportion of households also procured medicinal and herbal plants from their community forests. On the other hand, very few households procured timber from community forests even as substantial minorities of households claimed to obtain edible plants and livestock feeds from the forests. In terms of the importance households attached to key forest products as household use items; timber shows up as not important while water and firewood where very important.

With respect to firewood collection, respondents' conceptions of firewood went beyond freshly cut wood, dead branches, twigs, crop and plant residue (used for households' energy needs) to include the collection of tree woody biomass for home construction and fencing needs. Nevertheless, respondents were reluctant to admit to the harvesting of grown tree poles and to feel safe regarding such activities as firewood collection. For this reason, it was clear that community forests were a very important source of home construction materials for most households.

Livestock feeds referred to all non-woody herbaceous plants cut for animal feeds. It included members of the grass and sedge families, a variety of legumes, and other broad leaf plants. Close to a third of all households in our sample saw the forest as an important if not very important source of livestock feeds. Community forests were also cited by the majority (68.4 per cent) of respondents to be an important source of herbal/medicinal plants. The importance households attached to different forest products is collaborated by data on the proportions of households that procured these resources from the community forests.

As regards community forests acting as a major source of food products for the sample of households, field observations did not confirm this – even as some households had members who occasionally procured a few edible fruit (mangoes, guavas,) tubers (a variety of yam species) and mushrooms from community forests for home consumption. Most households did appear to meet their food needs through own-farm production.

However, given average household size of 5.9, one would have expected a statistically significant relation to exist between household land size and the importance of forests as an important source of food[22], which is not borne out as Table 8 below shows. Thus, disproportionately less individuals across all land size holdings considered community forests an important source of edible plants and more so among those individuals with land size holdings less than 5 acres.

Table 8. Association - land size holding and importance of community forests as a source of edible plants

Size of Land	Edible Plants Harvested as Household Use Item			Total
	Very important	Important	Not important	
<1 acre	10	14	29	53
	18.9%	26.4%	54.7%	100.0%
>1acre<5	17	20	87	124
	13.7%	16.1%	70.2%	100.0%
	16	23	40	79
>5acres	20.3%	29.1%	50.6%	100.0%
	16.8%	22.3%	60.9%	100.0%

Chi square = 9.016   p < 0.061

Concerning to the relation between the number of units of livestock held by the households and the importance households attached to community forests as a source of livestock feeds; no statistically significant relation were found, except for poultry (see Table 9). However, given the small number of livestock units held by almost all sampled households, and the fact that very little zero grazing was seen to be practiced with respect to higher value livestock such as goats and sheep, these findings are to be expected. Particularly with respect to high value livestock such as goats, these results should suggest that many are left to graze openly in community forests with dire consequences for reforestation efforts as is shown shortly.

Table 9. Associations – number of livestock by type and importance households attach to community forests as a source of livestock feeds

Livestock type	Chi square	P <
Cattle	5.387	0.250
Goat	27.393	0.197
Sheep	14.493	0.270
Poultry	81.125	0.000
Pigs	15.306	0.502

4.7 Restrictions in Community Forests

Respondents reported that there existed a variety of restrictions on product harvesting in community forests. Overall however, it was with respect to the harvesting of timber products that almost all respondents cited severe restrictions. According to respondents, restrictions on timber harvesting covered the gamut of outright bans on harvesting to quantity and maturity restrictions. For all other forest products except livestock feeds, almost all households reported no restrictions on harvest (see Table 10).

Table 10. Per cent of respondents citing restrictions on the harvesting of key community forest products

Timber	94.2%
Firewood	1.9%
Herbal/medicinal plants	1.2%
Water	0.8%
Edible plants	1.2%
Livestock feeds	33.7%

Close to 33.7 per cent of respondents cited severe restrictions on the harvesting of livestock feeds from community forests that ranged from outright bans to quantity restrictions. As can be seen from Table 11, over 40 per cent of respondents cited outright bans and quantity restrictions in respect of livestock feeds. Given the prevalence of non-zero grazing practices with respect to high value livestock, a ban on the grazing of livestock in community forests would appear to be aimed at promoting reforestation efforts. For example, it was observed in the field that the grazing of goats (which are kept by a substantial majority of households) was severely restricted in order that community based efforts at reforestation are not undermined. Also the nature of restrictions imposed on the harvest of timber highlight community efforts to ensure sustainable levels of harvest. Thus, though highly restricted, those able to obtain licenses to fell timber are subjected to severe quantity and product maturity restrictions.

Table 11. Per cent of households reporting their knowledge of the existence of different restrictions on the harvesting of various community forest products

Nature of Restrictions	Forest Products					
	Timber	Firewood	Herbal Plants	Water	Edible Plants	Livestock Feeds
Harvesting Banned	1.2%		0.4%		0.4%	41.9%
Quantity Restrictions	70.5%	0.8%	0.4%			46.1%
Maturity Restrictions	22.5%					0.4%
Traditional/Cultural Use Restrictions		0.4%	0.4%	0.4%	0.8%	0.4%
No Restrictions	5.0%	98.1%	98.1%	98.8%	98.1%	10.5%

4.8. Economic Importance of Community Forests to Households

The depth of resource extraction by households from community forests can be gauged by the frequency of harvest and time household members spend collecting, processing and transporting different products from community forest to house. On average household members visit the forests to extract water and firewood four and two times a week, respectively. The forests are visited less frequently with respect to the harvesting of the other forest resources. Nevertheless, one may be inclined to think that household members engage in the multiple harvesting of forest products at any one visit.

When frequency of harvest is linked to various measures of a household's economic position (land holding, value of farm implements), a statistically significant relation is found with respect to firewood and edible plants, in the case of land size holding, and timber, water and livestock feeds in the case of value of farm implements. With land size holding, it is plausible that those with less land are likely to visit community forests more often than their better endowed neighbours even, as earlier reported, community forests were not an important source of food for the majority of households. Thus, for land constrained households, the results here show that community forests may indeed be a fairly important source of food, with household members frequently visiting them to procure fruit and/or edible tubers.

However, it was also more likely, given the observed encroachment practices, that land poor households had members who were more likely to engage in charcoal burning and crop cultivation in community forests.[23] In the case of firewood, a plausible explanation is that less land endowed households may be more disposed to market firewood. While it was not possible to solicit credible responses as to which community forest products households marketed for cash[24], it was an open secret that some community members sold piles of firewood procured from community forests in the small towns that dot Budongo sub-county.

On the other hand, the fact that the frequencies of harvest of timber, and especially water and livestock feeds were statistically significant with respect to the possession of farm implements, is indicative of the constraint a lack of adequate farm implements imposes on households' abilities to efficiently extract these forest products. Thus, because the harvesting of these forest products requires the use of tools (i.e. axes (timber), jerry cans (water), machetes (livestock feeds)); *implements-poor* households may find a need to visit forests more frequently to obtain threshold levels of resources to meet household needs.[25]

In terms of drawing a link between time spent in collecting, processing and transporting different products from community forest to house and key household wealth ranks, statistical significance was established only with respect to water and a household's total values of productive assets. Again the implication is that though water is a very important resource households drew from community forests, it was those households that were more endowed with productive assets (probably more jerry cans) who were in a better position to exploit more of this resource.

On the other hand, when a broader definition of a household's wealth position, namely *value of total household assets* is pitted against a household's reliance on community forests as captured by the frequency of resource extraction; it is with respect to firewood, livestock feeds, and to a lesser degree water, that statistically significant relations are established. The implication here is that wealthier household's were more likely to enjoy greater benefits from community forests as imputed from their greater frequency of harvest of the more important forest resources.

However, with respect to time spent in collecting, processing and transporting forest products to house and a household's wealth position (i.e. *value of total household asset)*; a statistically significant relation was found only with respect to livestock feeds (see Table 12). This suggests that for wealthier households, the ownership of livestock does constitute a larger share of total household wealth, requiring these households to spend more time in the harvesting of livestock feeds from community forests. Overall these results appear to confirm the view that a household's wealth position says something about its dependence (and/or the levels of benefits it enjoys) on (from) community forests.

Table 12. Association-frequency of harvest, time spent in resource extraction and value of total household assets

Forest product	Frequency of harvest (per week) v/s household total assets		Time spent in harvest (hrs) v/s household total assets	
	Chi-square	Significance level	Chi-square	Significance level
Timber	4.365	0.627	5.688	0.841
Firewood	37.333	0.000	6.037	0.914
Herbal/medicinal plants	8.003	0.433	7.827	0.799
Water	20.830	0.106	15.130	0.369
Edible plants	8.782	0.361	7.447	0.281
Livestock feeds	28.815	0.000	11.952	0.018

4.9 Money Values of Community Forest Products to Households

Money values for community forest products were computed for firewood and water, which had readily available market prices.[26] On average, households extracted respectively, Ugandan shillings 672 and 2133 worth of water and firewood per week. Taking water as an example, and valuing a jerry can of water at Ugandan shillings 50, this translates to about 40 jerry cans of water procured per household per week. Given that each jerry contains 20 litres of water, a substantial majority of households would have at their disposal approximately. 800 litres of water a week or about 114 litres of water per day or about 19.3 litres of water per household member a day (i.e. average household size of 5.9 persons), which is slightly above the 13 litres per day National Surveys conducted in 1996 and 1999 found for rural inhabitants in Uganda.[27] Nevertheless, a substantial majority of households procured resources to the tune of less than Ugandan shillings 2000 per week of these forest resources.

In terms of linking a household's wealth position and the money values of water and firewood households procure from their community forests, almost equal proportions of households with varying land size holdings procure varying values of firewood in a week. When values for wood are cross tabulated with ranges of total household assets an almost similar picture emerges suggesting that overall irrespective of a household's wealth position, very little firewood resources in terms of value are extracted from community forests and that no one socio-economic group appears to have an edge over the other in terms of values (and by implication benefits) for firewood extracted from community forests.

As with firewood, a similar picture emerges with respect to water. Thus, large proportions of households with varying land size holdings procure water valued in the lower band. A similar situation replicates itself with respect to ranges of total household assets. Overall, these results suggest that households across all wealth rankings extract very little in terms of values where water and firewood are concerned (i.e. close to 71.5 per cent and 94.1 per cent of our sample of households extracted values of firewood and water of no more that Ugandan shillings 2000 per week in each case). When one views this in quantity terms, for firewood, this translates to two stacks (bundles) of firewood taking rural prices for firewood to be Ugandan shillings 1000. So unless some household members engage in the illegal cutting of tree stumps and tree poles under the pretext of collecting firewood, households' firewood extractive practices would appear not to be unsustainable where the preservation of community forests in the study areas is concerned.

4.10 Resource Appropriation Costs

4.10.1 Weekly Costs of Tools

An attempt was made to estimate the costs households incurred through the use of own tools to appropriate resources from their community forests. The formulae used, sought to divide the total value of tools held by households with their expected use life (in years) expressed as weekly cost of tools as shown below.

Weekly cost of tools = $\sum(C_i/(TL_i * WY))$

Where:
- C_i is the cost of tool i
- TL_i is the total use life for tool i in years
- WY = number of weeks in a year = 48

On average households expended approximately Ugandan shillings 506 per week in cost of tools, although as depicted in Table 13, a substantial minority of households with tools faced resource appropriation tools costs far in excess of this average. From Table 14 it is clear that when a households' wealth position in terms of total productive assets owned is evaluated vis-à-vis the range of weekly cost of tools, disproportionately more household in the poor and rich categories face tools appropriation costs less than 500, and between 500 and 1000 Ugandan shillings respectively. This suggests that poor (rich) households face lower (higher) tools appropriation costs because they hold few (more) productive assets or tools respectively.

Table 13. Number (per cent) of households that incur varying range values in costs of tools for resource extraction (weekly costs)

Range cost of tools (Ugandan shillings)	Number (%)
Costs < 500	138 (54.1)
500 < costs < 1000	105 (41.2)
Costs >1000	12 (4.7)
Total	**255 (100)**

On the other hand, it could also be argued that middle wealth and rich households ought to face lower tools appropriation costs. This is because their greater assets should allow a more flexible use of their tools. The greater wealth should allow them to have others, possibly members from poorer households procure forest resources for them (water, firewood, etc.) and thus reduce on their use of own-tools to procure community forest resource which, in turn, should mean higher weekly tools costs for households that are tools poor.

Table 14. Association - range of cost of tools and key household socio-economic variables

Range cost of tools versus range values of total productive assets

Range cost of tools	Values < 30,000	30,000<values < 65,000	Values >65,000	Total
Costs <-500	100.0%	48.7%	0%	54.1%
500<costs < 1000	0%	51.3%	70.0%	41.2%
Costs >1000	0%	0%	30.0%	4.7%

4.10.2 Community Forest Product Appropriation Costs

An attempt was made to estimate the resource appropriation costs that households faced with respect to the key products they procured from their community forests. The costs were obtained as the product of: time spent in collecting, processing and transporting the relevant resource to house; quantities harvested; and the rural hourly wage rate, which was taken to be Ugandan shillings 200. On average households incur greater opportunity costs in terms of rural wages foregone in the extraction of water. This is followed albeit distantly, by firewood extraction. On average household appropriation costs across all forest products were 1651 Ugandan shillings. When weekly costs of tools are included, average weekly appropriation costs facing households across all community forest products rise to 2157 Ugandan shillings.

Also, across all wealth rankings, close to three-fourths of sampled households faced total resource appropriation costs not exceeding Ugandan shillings 2000 per week. Statistically, the relations between a household's wealth position and community forest appropriation costs was most significant with respect to the range of values of productive assets (tools) and total household assets. Intuitively, these results appear logical given that water and firewood were the main products households procured from their community forests. So even while the harvesting of these resources involved the use of traditional technologies; collecting, processing and transporting them to house can be expected to be time intensive for some households.[28]

4.11 Households' Oversight Functions in Community Forestry

Save for timber, for which felling needs to be sanctioned, all other forest products are harvested free by all. In their substantial majorities, respondents reported that their community forests were more or less open access resources; open to individuals they (respondents) regarded as 'outsiders, namely: non-community members, commercial loggers, charcoal burners, etc. The majority of respondents also cited the lack of institutional frameworks to deny 'outsiders' access rights to their community forests.

However, through a number of initiatives for community forestry, households have come to appreciate the need to police the proper use of their community forests. Thus, over 67.4 per cent of respondents claimed to participate in some oversight activities with respect to 'others' use of community forest resources. These oversight or monitoring activities included, but were not limited to activities such as, reporting transgression (i.e. others resource misuse activities) and/or on the condition of forest resources to the relevant authorities, in this case the NFA (see Table 15).

Table 15. Number (per cent) of respondents claiming to undertake various tasks in community forestry

	Number	%
Do not undertake any oversight duties	84	32.6
Reporting transgressions to relevant authorities	127	49.2
Observing others resource harvesting practices	38	14.7
Reporting on the condition of forest resources to relevant authorities	5	1.9
Other oversight duties	4	1.6
Total	256	100

For those respondents who claimed not to participate in any oversight activities, corruption and illegal practices (the felling of timber, charcoal burning, crop cultivation, etc,) that are sometimes sanctioned by governmental forestry departments/officials appear to have eroded their interest in undertaking any community based oversight functions in community forests. There was also the general belief among many respondents that collaborative forest management initiatives were earmarked for degraded forest reserves and that there was nothing left to share in the form of benefits.

The role politicians play in stifling collaborative forest management initiatives was also raised by many respondents. In responding to the demands of their electorates, many local politicians are seen to undermine community forestry initiatives by sanctioning and abetting the actions of those who encroached on community forests. For example, NFA officials did note that community forestry efforts in the study areas have come under great pressure from Internally Displaced Persons (IDPs) from the war ravaged northern districts of Uganda and the rebel affected districts of Bundibugyo and Kasese in western Uganda.

Overall, there appeared in practice to exist some indifference among respondents as regards their oversight roles in community forestry. Table 16 shows that respondents in their majorities held the view that oversight duties in community forestry were the responsibility of forestry department (NFA) guards, community appointed guards or a combination of these guards. Very few respondents admitted to being aware that they as community and/or CLA members had primary and specific roles in monitoring others actions in community forests. An equally small number of respondents admitted to not being sure who actually was responsible for oversight functions in community forests.

Table 16. Respondents knowledge about who is accountable for oversight duties in community forests

	Number	%
NFA guards	33	12.8
Community appointed guards	55	21.3
Any combination of the preceding modes	157	60.9
Community members	7	2.7
No one	6	2.4
Total	258	100.0

The preponderance of respondents view that community forest oversight functions were mostly the responsibility of the NFA may flow from the way they understood fees charged for felling timber were used. While community members were not charged fees for resource harvest, many held the view that forestry officials did charge 'outsiders' some fees for felling timber, poles and livestock feeds (mostly elephant grass used as cattle feeds). When asked to specifically state to which use forestry officials put levied funds, the majority (i.e., over ¾ of respondents) understood these payments to finance a combination of three activities, namely resource use monitoring, community mobilization for community forestry and reforestation activities. Nevertheless, about one-fifth of respondents claimed not to know to which use these fees were put. All in all, respondents must have viewed levied fees as sufficient to finance any oversight functions in community forestry, and likewise, to lessen their assumed oversight roles in community forestry.

4.12 Rule Design, Participation and Community Forestry

All respondents admitted to being aware of community based forest management initiatives in their communities. Some like BUCODO's initiatives, in addition, were understood as seeking to initiate broader income generating and community development projects to reduce households' dependence on community forests. Nevertheless, BUCODO's sensitization efforts for sustainable community forestry were also understood by the majority of respondents to involve the establishment of rules to allocate benefits and costs of resource use and management, to promote community input in the design of these rules and in creating platforms for conflict resolution where forest resource use and management was concerned.

Overall, respondents understood the design of resources use and management rules to emanate from cooperative and participatory community based governance structures (Local Council, CLA) and formal government institutions such as the NFA. Table 17 presents the number and percentage of respondents and their awareness of the institutional frameworks from which community forest use and management rules were sourced. Nevertheless, despite respondents having a wide level of awareness of community forestry initiatives in their communities, a substantial number of them (16.7 per cent) were not aware of the source of many of the existing rules regarding the use and management of their community forests. Equally perplexing is the large proportion (26.6 per cent) of respondents who were of the view that the NFA was the principal source of these rules, suggesting that despite great efforts to sensitization communities for community forestry, many community members still see a domineering role for the NFA in the forestry sector.

Table 17. Respondents knowledge of institutions responsible for community forest use and management rules design

	Number	per cent
Village Local Council	2	.8
Village CLA meetings	33	12.9
Forest department, NFA officials/offices	68	26.6
Any combination of the above institutional structures	110	43.0
Don't know	43	16.8
Total	256	100.0

Nevertheless, about 195 (75.6 per cent) respondents claimed that they and/or members of their households actively participated in community forestry activities initiated within the institutional frameworks depicted in Table 17. The depth of respondents' participation is evident when one considers that of these, 189, 131 and 123 claimed to regularly attend village meetings aimed at addressing general forestry issues, to undertake forestry resource monitoring activities and to commit time towards activities aimed at resolving resource use and management conflicts respectively.

Across the sample, respondents were satisfied with the way resource use and management rules where designed. However, 4 (1.6 per cent) respondents were dissatisfied on account of local leaders/elites dominance of deliberations; 3 (1.2 per cent) respondents on account of discriminative practices that did not seriously consider the interests and views of less vocal community members; 4 (1.6 per cent) respondents who felt that local government and forestry offices/officials dominated the rules design process, and 6 (2.6 per cent) respondents who were dissatisfied on account of any combination of the preceding reasons. Finally, almost all respondents were satisfied with rules design as they related to individual forest products, although a few did express a desire to see a relaxation of restrictions on the harvesting of tree poles for home construction.

However, despite these general low levels of dissatisfaction with the way community forestry use and management rules are designed, some respondents did cite specific grievances. Thus, some felt that within their Local Councils and CLA some self-seeking individuals attained leadership, which they then held on for extended periods of time only later becoming proxy representatives of the NFA. Quickly problems of conflict of interest emerge, which undermine the whole concept of collaborative forest management. Some female respondents also suggested that gender and equality were mere formalities under community forestry initiatives and tended to serve the interests of the NFA. Thus, equal participation, fairness and sharing of benefits usually left a lot to be desired. Males were also said to still dominate and occupy most key decision-making positions in community forestry initiatives.

The difficulties faced to institute effective community forestry initiatives and garner the full participation of community members in the study areas also flow from weaknesses in the policy and legal frameworks that underpin CFM in Uganda. First, the 2001 Forestry Policy provides for CFM but not community based forest management. With CFM, communities are only obliged to collaborate with "responsible bodies", in this case, the NFA. The law only accords communities "responsible body" status when it comes to establishment of community forests and private forests on land that is communally or privately owned respectively. The constraints inherent in this policy immediately create operational bottlenecks.

For example, NFA officials argued that whereas the policy sought to promote community participation in forest management on government and private forest land, presently participatory forest management initiatives have been focused on Central Forest Reserves such as Budongo forest, which come under NFA supervision. In the study sites this focus has meant that pressure has been exerted on the NFA in terms of capacity to meet community demands for greater access to forest resources. Also, a time consuming and uncertain nine-stage process has to be followed by communities applying for CFM (see Table 18).

Table 18. CMF Process

Step 1	Initiating the process
Step 2	Preparing an application for CMF
Step 3	Meeting between applicant and responsible body
Step 4	Participatory situation analysis
Step 5	Initial negotiation and drafting of a CFM plan
Step 6	Institutional formation and development
Step 7	Continuation of negotiations
Step 8	Review of the plan and agreement by stakeholders
Step 9	Implementation

For example, it was evident that NFA lacked the resources to undertake community mobilization and sensitization programmes for community forestry in the study areas. NFA officials at the Nyabyeya office admitted to lacking the capacity to implement community forestry activities given their budgetary and staffing constraints. They also pointed out that sensitization for CFM needed to encompass a whole range of stakeholders, especially top NFA officials who in the main tended to be skeptical about community forestry initiatives. They saw these initiatives as empowering communities (through the transfer of property rights and control of forest resources to communities) to indulge in illegal activities rather than implement agreed to plans.

Delays in the in the signing of CFM agreements was also cited as causing apathy towards community forestry initiatives in the study communities. For example, in the whole of Budongo sub-county, only one CLA (in Kasenene parish) had finalized the formal process of registering a CLA. BUCODO officials did cite problems with district land registries with respect to why other CLA in the sub-county had as yet to formally register their CLA. They did point out that these delays led to almost open access resource use in designated community forests.

BUCODO officials also highlighted the fact that the management of Community Forests was regulated by the National Forestry and Tree Planting Act while the establishment of Community Land Associations was regulated under the Land Act. This dichotomy caused management delays because the implementation of the Land Act has been slow and yet the gazettement of Community Forests depends upon an established Communal Land Association (CLA).

The lack of information and its dissemination to communities about the available opportunities in participatory forest management was also highlighted. While Section 91 of the National Forestry and Tree Planting Act 2003 provides for access to information on forest products and services, more often than not, such information does not trickle down to community members[29].

More significant is the fact that where CFM agreements have been signed, they have been drafted in English with very few community members being able to comprehend their contents. The issues contained therein are therefore not appropriately deciphered. This has proved a major hindrance during the negotiation and implementation stages of the CFM process. Chances of communities getting distorted information are also high. This provides a window for manipulation of the unsuspecting communities by self seeking and opportunistic CFM leaders. In addition, communities can not hire offices and staff; therefore their documents are kept with the Chairperson and this establishes an additional barrier of access to information.

Also failure to recognize the value of forest resources has led to critical lack of extension and/or advisory service provision to communities. Thus communities have preferred enterprises with immediate returns (piggery, poultry, maize, beans). Communities have little motivation to indulge in long-term activities that involves planting, growing and protecting trees. It may also be true that given the high levels of poverty in the study areas, immediate needs like medical bills and basic household requirements are a motivation for enterprises with quick returns. Nevertheless, it is also true that demand-driven forestry extension service delivery has failed and communities have received little advice from the National Agricultural Advisory Services (NAADS).

NFA and BUCODO officials also highlighted the fact that CFM Agreements have a life span of 10 years yet many forestry activities are of a longer gestation period. For example trees take 20 years and above to mature yet private tree farmers in Central Forest Reserves are given permits of up to 50 years. This dichotomy was said to create disincentives for communities to undertake long-term and lucrative investments under community forestry by restricting themselves to subsistence tendencies (collection of mushrooms, rattan and hunting).

Gender and equality was also highlighted as a mere formality under CFM agreement; it being intended to serve the interests of the "Responsible Body" (NFA) as a counterpart to the agreement. Equal participation, fairness and sharing of benefits leave a lot to desire with women and the elderly falling victims to this inequity. Particularly for women, inequities can be attributed to a patriachical cultural milieu in the study areas, which marginalizes women in decision and resource sharing both at the household and community levels. Persons with disabilities, the old and vulnerable groups (i.e. children, the youth, etc.) are equally marginalized where the sharing of information about CFM is concerned.

Finally, BUCODO officials talked of a general failure by decision makers (including national and local politicians) to recognize the value of forest resources and attaching low priority to community forestry initiatives. Political interference by government officials and local politicians who directly support encroachments in community forests have made communities skeptical about community forestry initiatives and to dampen morale and the speed at which initiatives are implemented. Political interference has also resulted in a lack of respect for professionalism in the forest sector, and CBO voice and opinion.

The current interface between local authorities, CLAs and communities in the study areas also has implications for how the latter's incentives for community forestry can be engendered and sustained. It is important to note that CLAs are extremely young institutions and are being implemented without government support or significant funding. Also it is too early to judge the authority of CLAs as recognized by local communities. However, it is unclear if communities respect CLAs or believe they have the power to produce positive outcomes.

For example, CLA officers view enforcement of resource access and use as a central role. They stop outsiders from illegally accessing the forest or chopping down tress, but often pay a heavy price. CLA members have been challenged and physically attacked when trying to enforce rules. Also while patrols identify instances of illegal use, the areas in which CLAs can enforce use are minimal.[30]

This evidence suggests that local communities are more likely to recognize the authority of local institutions such as LCs and other traditional forms of authority, if the institutions provide tangible benefits to the community, regardless of the official authority vested in them.[31] Because CLAs are neither a direct nor a representative democracy, they appear to represent the most inequitable form of access for communities to forest resources. For example, ten representatives are chosen through an informal election process to work with BUCODO to draft a CLA constitution for the community forest. Meetings are held with community members but do not include all affected stakeholder groups or ensure equal voting powers.

Also, CLAs are not upwardly accountable to any official government body although they are upwardly accountable to BUCODO for funding, training, and other forms of logistical support. However, CLA officials/members live in the communities and as such are subject to an informal form of peer pressure. Thus, while CLAs currently have no revenue schemes in place, there are plans to ensure that local communities receive a portion of forest resources CLAs currently raise from fines to outsiders who enter forests and extract anything, even non-timber forest products. much of this money now goes to forest management schemes, such as purchasing seedlings to replace destroyed trees and none to community members engaged in community forestry initiatives.

4.13 Household's Wealth Position and Participation in Community Forestry

As pertains to the question of whether a household's wealth position has some relation to its members being engaged in community forestry activities. Table 19 shows that when households are evaluated along the range of values of total household assets. In their majorities, respondents claimed to participate or to have household members participate in community forestry activities. In addition, participation appears to become more pronounced as one moves up along this range (i.e. disproportionately more households in the higher income ranges participated in community forestry activities).

Table 19. Association between household members' participation in community forestry activities and range for total household assets

Household participate in forest use and management institutional formation	Range for total household assets			Total
	Assets < 100,000	100,000 < assets < 500,000	Assets >500,000	
No	21	39	1	61
	35.0%	21.0%	10.0%	23.8%
Yes	39	147	9	195
	65.0%	79.0%	90.0%	76.2%
Total	60	186	10	256
	100.0%	100.0%	100.0%	100.0%

Chi–square = 6.0018   p< 0.05

With respect to respondents' the result confirms the preceding finding by establishing a statistically significant relation between participation and a household's wealth position. Thus, whether participation relates to attending village meetings for community forestry, forest monitoring activities or resource sanctioning and conflict resolution activities, disproportionately more households participate in the higher wealth echelons than in the lower ones when households are evaluated on the basis of values of total household assets.

4.14 Household Time in Community Forestry

On average our sample of households committed 1.99, 2.15 and 1.19 hours a week to attend village forestry meetings, monitor forestry resource use, and in resolving resource use and management conflicts respectively. When time spent in the various tasks of community forestry were cross tabulated with a key household socio-economic indicator (i.e. range values of total household assets) the relation was statistically significant with respect to resource monitoring. Overall, however, disproportionately more poor households were likely to commit less time to community forestry activities than their richer counterparts..

Table 20 provides the distribution of ranges of time spent weekly by household members in various community forestry activities. The majority of respondents spent less than two hours in the various functions of: attending village meetings for community forestry, community forestry monitoring, and conflict resolution around the use and a management of community forests. Except for time spent in conflict resolution, substantial minorities of households also had members who spent between three and five hours in community forestry activities. Very few households had members who committed more than five hours in community forestry activities.

Table 20. Number (per cent) of respondents and/or their household members reporting committing varying levels of time in community forestry activities

Range of Hours	Village meetings Number (per cent)	Resource monitoring Number (per cent)	Attend sanctioning/conflict resolution Number (per cent)
Hours < 2	131 (51.2)	144 (56.3)	207 (80.9)
3 <hours < 5	125 (48.8)	92 (35.9)	47 (18.4)
Hours > 5		20 (7.8)	2 (0.8)
Total	256	256	256

4.15 Household Transaction Costs in Community Forestry

To calculate the imputed money value of transaction costs households incur in community forestry, household total time committed to undertaking the various tasks in community forestry was multiplied by the village hourly wage rate, which was taken to be Ugandan shillings 200. Table 21 below provides average values in Ugandan shillings of transaction costs households face in the various tasks underpinning community forestry in a week. Overall households face greater transaction costs in community forest monitoring tasks.

Table 21. Mean values of transaction costs households face in the various community forestry activities (Uganda shillings)

	Mean	Std. Deviation
Transaction costs for village meetings	398.44	272.673
Transaction costs in monitoring	429.69	465.325
Transaction costs in sanction/conflict resolution	238.28	299.443
Total transaction costs in community forestry	1066.41	889.748

In addition, as Table 22 shows, the majority of households face weekly transaction costs in community forestry not exceeding Ugandan shillings 1200. A substantial minority nevertheless face costs in the range of 1200 and 2200 shillings, while very few households face costs in excess of 2200 Ugandan shillings. Overall, for those who actually participate in community forestry activities, almost 90 per cent face weekly transaction costs not exceeding Ugandan shillings 2200.

Table 22. Number and per cent of households facing varying ranges of transaction costs in community forestry

Range of Costs	Number (per cent) Total sample	Number (per cent) Participating households
Transaction costs <1,200	144 (56.3)	81 (42.0)
1200< Transaction costs < 2200	90 (35.2)	90 (47.0)
Transaction costs> 2200	22 (8.6)	22 (11.0)
Total	256	193

4.16 Transaction Costs by Household Wealth Rankings

When transaction costs are broken down by a household's wealth position, results are mixed. When land size holding is the category of interest, rich households are shown to face the highest level of transaction costs in community forestry. Thus, the imputed value of weekly transaction costs rich households face in community forestry equal Ugandan shillings 1182. They are closely followed by poor households and then middle wealth households. When the value of total household assets is the variable of interest, still rich households face higher transaction costs and again when total value of productive assets is the variable of interest.

All in all, it would appear that richer households face higher transaction costs in community forestry compared to middle wealth and poor households (see Table 23). However, because richer households had members who were more likely to spend more time in community forestry activities, it follows that these households were also more likely to incur greater transactions costs in these activities than their poorer neighbours.

Table 23. Mean values of transaction costs households face by wealth rankings

Transaction Costs

Land size holding

Wealth ranking categories	Mean
Poor: land < 1 acres	1102
Middle wealth: 1<acres<5	977
Rich: land > 5 acres	1182

Total household assets

Wealth ranking categories	Mean
Poor: assets < 100,000	637
Middle wealth: 100,000 <assets < 500,000	1185
Rich: assets > 500,000	1440

Total value of productive tools

Wealth ranking categories	Mean
Poor: assets < 30,000	1041
Middle wealth: 30,000< assets<65,000	1012
Rich: assets > 65,000	1265

Thus, richer households were more likely to engage and commit more time in community forestry activities than poorer households and invariably to face higher transaction costs. However, it was also the richer households that were shown to benefit more from the community forests given their greater frequencies of resource extraction and/or greater possession of productive tools to effect greater resource extraction. For poor households, the imperatives of basic survival pointed to the incentives facing such households to undertake crop farming and other illegal activities (i.e. timber felling, charcoal burning, etc.) in community forests mostly because they lacked key productive assets such as land.

4.17 Resource Appropriation Costs by Household Wealth Rankings

On the other hand, when households' total resource appropriation costs in community forests are assigned as per household wealth position, poor households now face the highest costs. In all categories of wealth ranking, poor households faced higher appropriation costs; more so when land size holding was the variable of interest (see Table 24). Overall, poorer households should be expected to incur higher appropriation costs, given their lower asset bases (especially of productive tools), whose values in use are rapidly amortized over time.

Table 24. Mean values of appropriation costs households face by wealth rankings

Appropriation Costs

Land size holding

Wealth ranking categories	Mean
Poor: land < 1 acres	3356
Middle wealth: 1<acres<5	1777
Rich: land > 5 acres	2006

Total household assets

Wealth ranking categories	Mean
Poor: assets < 100,000	2668
Middle wealth: 100,000 <assets < 500,000	1981
Rich: assets > 500,000	2495

Total value of productive tools

Wealth ranking categories	Mean
Poor: assets < 30,000	2795
Middle wealth: 30,000< assets<65,000	1787
Rich: assets > 65,000	2610

4.18 Transaction Costs as Share of Appropriation Costs

Table 25 presents results for transaction costs as a share of total resource appropriation costs households with different socio-economic status incur in community forestry. It is clear that transaction costs as a share of total resource appropriation costs are higher for rich and middle income household across all categories of wealth rankings.[32] In fact, when the value of total household assets (possibly a better gauge of a household's wealth position) is the variable of interest, households with total household wealth in excess of 100,000 Ugandan shillings appear to incur three times as much as households with total household assets of less than 100,000 Ugandan shillings. The implication is that when transaction costs in community forestry are evaluated as a share of the costs of forest resource extraction, wealthier households share a heavier burden of the former costs than their poorer counterparts.

Table 25. Transaction costs as a share of total resource appropriation costs by wealth rankings

Land size holding	
Wealth ranking categories	**Proportion**
Poor: land < 1 acres	0.3
Middle wealth: 1<acres<5	0.5
Rich: land > 5 acres	0.6
Total household assets	
Wealth ranking categories	**Proportion**
Poor: assets < 100,000	0.2
Middle wealth: 100,000 <assets < 500,000	0.6
Rich: assets > 500,000	0.6
Total value of productive tools	
Wealth ranking categories	**Proportion**
Poor: assets < 30,000	0.4
Middle wealth: 30,000< assets<65,000	0.6
Rich: assets > 65,000	0.5

As suggested in the literature, transaction costs of collective action at the community level are influenced by the physical characteristics of a resource and social capital of community members (see section 2.5.2). Many of what are regarded as community forests in the study areas were in fact depleted of timber and undergrowth and encroached with crop cultivation. As a consequence it is those households with threshold levels of tools and assets that where more likely to affect appreciable levels of resource extraction albeit at higher costs. In this regard the higher proportion of transaction costs as a share of appropriation costs for richer households is immediately implied.

4.19 Value of Benefits Households Accrue from Community Forests by Wealth Rankings.

Earlier it was stated that water and firewood were the key main forest resources that household procured from their community forests, and ones to which realistically, values could be attached. Table 26 shows weekly values for these two resources that households procure from their community forests defined by various household wealth rank categories. Overall no disenable differences in values are evident except that rich households appear to benefits much more than their middle income and poor households.

Table 26. Mean values of benefits households derive from their community forests by wealth rankings

Land size holding	
Wealth ranking categories	**Mean**
Poor: land < 1 acres	2581
Middle wealth: 1<acres<5	2476
Rich: land > 5 acres	3470
Total household assets	
Wealth ranking categories	**Mean**
Poor: assets < 100,000	2615
Middle wealth: 100,000 <assets < 500,000	2860
Rich: assets > 500,000	2905
Total value of productive tools	
Wealth ranking categories	**Mean**
Poor: assets < 30,000	2582
Middle wealth: 30,000< assets<65,000	2658
Rich: assets > 65,000	3749

4.20 Transaction Costs as Share of Total Benefits from Community Forests

Table 27 presents results for transaction costs as a share of total value of benefits for households ranked along various wealth categories.[33] Here again no discernable pattern is evident distinguishing shares by household socio-economic position. It would be a fair assumption looking at these shares to assert that across all households, transaction costs as a share of the value of total benefits household obtain from their community forests is the same. In a sense, it would appear that all sampled households derive the same benefits given the costs they incur in community forestry.

Table 27. Transaction costs as a proportion of total value of benefits households derive from community forests by wealth rankings

Land size holding	
Wealth ranking categories	**Proportion**
Poor: land < 1 acres	0.4
Middle wealth: 1<acres<5	0.4
Rich: land > 5 acres	0.3
Total household assets	
Wealth ranking categories	**Proportions**
Poor: assets < 100,000	0.2
Middle wealth: 100,000 <assets < 500,000	0.4
Rich: assets > 500,000	0.5
Total value of productive tools	
Wealth ranking categories	**Proportion**
Poor: assets < 30,000	0.4
Middle wealth: 30,000< assets<65,000	0.4
Rich: assets > 65,000	0.3

4.21 Net Benefits from Community Forestry by Household Wealth Rankings

Net benefits from community forestry are taken here to refer to the difference between the shares of transaction costs to total benefits and total appropriation costs. Table 28 shows that households across all wealth ranking categories suffer 0 or negative net benefits from CFM initiatives in their communities. What these results seem to suggest is that when transaction costs of CFM are evaluated in terms of their benefits to households (i.e. the benefits that accrue from sustainable resource use and managements) and the costs households face in appropriating community forest resources, an incentive exists for household members to engage in greater resource appropriations than to engage in those activities that ensure sustainable resource uses (i.e. those activities that underpin CFM).

Table 28. Net proportions – Difference of transaction costs as a share of total benefits and as share of total appropriation costs

Wealth ranking categories	Proportion
Land size holding	
Poor: land < 1 acres	0.1
Middle wealth: 1<acres<5	-0.1
Rich: land > 5 acres	-0.3
Total household assets	
Wealth ranking categories	Proportions
Poor: assets < 100,000	0.0
Middle wealth: 100,000 <assets < 500,000	-0.2
Rich: assets > 500,000	-0.1
Total value of productive tools	
Wealth ranking categories	Proportions
Poor: assets < 30,000	0.0
Middle wealth: 30,000< assets<65,000	-0.2
Rich: assets > 65,000	-0.2

Critical to an understanding of why across all sampled households no net benefits from community forestry initiatives were observed, lies in the fact that sampled households, despite the categorizations assigned them, were all equally positioned in the way transaction costs factored into the benefits and costs of their community forestry activities. For this reason, it was difficult to draw a clear link between the effects of transaction costs on community forestry initiatives across households by socio-economic status. Nevertheless, the finding that all households in the sample suffered 0 or negative net benefits, suggests that, as conceived in this study, transaction costs have very little effect on whether a household (or its members), irrespective of its socio-economic status engages with community forestry activities.

The negligible net benefits households derive from community forestry can also be linked to predominant views held by respondents that highlight the lack of tangible benefits from community forestry and the lack of guidelines for benefit sharing. For example, there was a preponderance of the view among respondents that the proceeds of sales of timber (confiscated from illegal fellers or levies on those felling timber legally) and eco-tourism activities were not passed on to community members most active in policing community forests. This view was echoed by some NFA officials who pointed out that current community forestry initiatives exhibit an asymmetry between household's burden of roles/responsibilities and benefits even as the NFA had come to depend on community members to police the forests.

Also, while resource sharing is provided for in the forestry policy, there are no guidelines for forest-benefit sharing. Quite often communities are left with low value items (mushrooms, water ponds, medicinal species, etc.). The high value products (reserved timber species and revenue from forestry services such as eco-tourism) are maintained by the Responsible Body (NFA). The CFM Agreement for Hanga-Kidwera community in Masindi district for example says, in part:

> Local inhabitants are privileged to obtain free of charge and in reasonable quantities to the discretion of the forest officer, bush firewood, bush poles, timber from unreserved tree species and sand for domestic use only. Domestic animals are allowed to visit water and salt lick points in the reserve.

5. CONCLUSION AND RECOMMENDATIONS

In conclusion it is clear that when transaction costs in community forestry are evaluated as the difference of their share in the benefits and costs of resource appropriation from community forests, households in the study areas appear to face few incentives to engage in community forestry. This conclusion emanates from the fact that:

1. The low state of social capital in the study areas, which is linked to the preponderance of migrants and IDPs, hinders community members' participation in community forestry, undermines the authority of traditional leaders to mobilize communities for collective action and invariably raises transaction costs in community forestry;

2. Poverty (i.e. the low average values of wealth held by households), which for very marginal households presents incentives for engaging in unsustainable community forest use and management practices such as crop cultivation and charcoal burning;

3. The need by marginal households to diversify their productive activities, which in the absence of diversification opportunities translates into unsustainable community forest use and management practices;

4. The lack of incentives facing more marginal households for community forestry, which flow from the high forest resource appropriation costs they face because they lack threshold levels of assets (tools) to effectively harvest, process and transport community forest resources to house;

5. Disincentives more marginal households face to participate in community forestry on account of corrupt and illegal practices sanctioned by forestry officials and politicians in community forests, discriminatory practices against marginal groups (women,

the disabled) and the domination of community forestry initiatives by local leaders and community elites;
6. The failure of CLAs to be fully democratic and accountable to forest dependent communities;
7. The low level of monetary values households derive from community forests with regard to the forest resources derived therein; and
8. Institutional and policy bottlenecks around community forestry initiatives that fail to effectively facilitate communities for community forestry by transforming communities, from positions as subordinate beneficiaries who receive minimal benefits from community forests, into positions where they themselves regulate this source of livelihood and with longer-term perspectives.

It is obvious that continuing CFM as it now exists in the study areas is not enough if community forests are to be revitalized and made to continue to support the livelihoods of those who live around them. Emphasis should be placed on efforts seeking to reorient community forestry initiatives towards a truly benefit-oriented and equitable model of people's participation in forest management. This will require:

a) Restating the basic premises of Collaborative Forest Management by paying more attention to operationalizing guidelines for forest benefit sharing, transfer of property rights, registration of CLAs and declaration of Community Forests;

b) The capacity of state agencies, such as the Forestry Inspection Division and NFA for CFM, should be built up by government by increasing manpower and other resources to the agencies. Government should also undertake to establish Forestry Committees, which are provided for in the National Forestry and Tree Planting Act as more inclusive forums for all community members, to discuss issues around CFM and to counter some of the inequities of power and voice inherent in CFM initiatives conceived under the rubric of CLAs;

c) Advocacy work to sensitize sceptical forest resource managers like the NFA about the need to transfer property rights and control of forest resources to communities by demonstrating to them that communities are capable of managing these resources. To this end, CBOs like BUCODE may need to invest in those initiatives that build social capital in communities, and the asset bases of households, in order to engender community members' greater participation in community forestry by lowering transaction costs faced therein;

d) Sufficient and user-friendly information in the vernacular be packaged and disseminated to forest dependent communities.

Similarly, the NFA should endeavour to translate CFM Agreements into vernacular languages in order to provide an opportunity for community members to fully understand their commitments under the agreements and avoid being manipulated by their CLA leaders;

e) BUCODO to promote measures that streamline gender and equity issues in CFM Agreements, CLAs and community forestry activities. To this end communities should be made to appreciate the need to empower women, the elderly and other vulnerable groups for community forestry as one way to allow for equal participation, fairness and sharing of benefits, and also as a way of building social capital in communities;

f) The greater development of grassroots networks of civil societies/NGOs/CBOs that work to build the assets (both social and physical) of economically marginal households and individuals. Such networks should help develop both the capacity of communities to implement collaborative approaches and the capacity of "Responsible Bodies" (NFA) to implement such approaches; and

g) Advocacy work to be stepped up at policy level to influence government on good governance issues in the forest sector, the role of both the political and civil leadership, accountability of responsible institutions, and collaborative forest management. There is need for civil society to influence government plans to incorporate collaborative forest management issues in overall government priority plans.

In conclusion, the study has established that transaction costs do indeed entail adverse effects for CFM in the study areas, and that these effects may differ for households on account of their socio-economic characteristics. Thus, while literature may suggest that the shifting of central government control over natural resource management to communities as with CLAs, *a prior,* should lead to more efficient management and improvements in the conditions of such resources; here a number of intervening constraints far beyond households' characteristics present mixed results. The state of social capital has been shown to play an important factor in stifling participation for community forestry, with the legal and regulatory regimes underpinning CFM equally proving less promotive of CFM.

Therefore, from an institutional economics perspective, it is clear that measures which seek to garner the participation of communities in CFM, but underplay the importance of well functioning institutions (i.e., rules and regulations underpinning CFM, local and traditional governance structures and their roles in building community social capital, democratic and accountable CLAs, etc) are bound to fail. The success of CFM initiatives in the study areas therefore calls for measures to strengthen all manner of institutions that promote community cooperation and participation for community forestry, and in particular measures to improve household income and asset bases to lower transaction costs in community forestry.

Endnotes

1. National Forests and Tree Planting Act 2003 and the National Forest Policy
2. The Land Act 1998 (cap 227) of Uganda
3. PFM refers to all forest management schemes where all stakeholders actively participate in the sustainable use and management of forest resources.
4. Ministry of Water Lands and Environment, [The 2001 Forestry Policy]
5. Prior to 1995, management and ownership of forests in Uganda rested with the national government.
6. See Wade (1988); Bromley and Cernea (1989); Ostrom (1990); Oakerson (1992); Tang (1992); Bardhan (1993); Nugent (1993); Uphoff (1993); Agrawal (2001).
7. For example, the LENF programme in Nigeria (Saarela-Kaonga 2001), the Malawi programmes (Mauambeta 2000), the Ijum-Kilum Project in Cameroon (Gardner et al. 2001), Arabuko-Sokoke Project in Kenya, the Chinyunyu Project in Zambia (Lukama 2000) and the Kabore Tambi Park project in Burkina Faso (Nana 2000).
8. For example, in Ghana forest-local populations are contracted to clear boundaries and paid to tend tree seedlings in forest reserves (Asare 1998). Also as a whole, community forestry in Francophone Sahel is strongly oriented towards providing labour opportunities and income rather than forest ownership or management rights (Ribot 1999).
9. A significant exception is Ivory Coast, where the land law of 1998 stipulates that all properties that are not registered within three (now ten) years will be deemed state property and subject to reallocation (Stamm 2000).
10. Forest Act of Tanzania 2002, clause 30 (4).
11. It is such elites who have the clout and means to take most advantage of an insecurely tenured forest. For example, they often possess the resources (equipment and labour) to illegally harvest, build new homesteads, clear new fields or establish mining activities in the forests. Policies and legislation which clarify and embed common tenure as a common interest asset and one that is equally co-owned among all members seem to do a great deal towards limiting casual or more directed encroachment and subdivision of the forest (see Alden Wily 1997; Alden Wily and Dewees 2001, and Gardiner 2003 for Cameroon and Kubsa 2002 for Ethiopia).

12. The US Federal Forest Service (2004) lists 'values of urban trees' to include psychological and aesthetic values, social values, historic values, environmental values, control over climate and air pollution and noise, protection of soil and water quality, and also monetary values.

13. She is establishing the hypothesis that CPR institutions follow the principle of "restraint for gain". If users are able to agree on what rules should be operative, it becomes possible to take advantage of such renewable resources such as fish stocks when they are well developed and, therefore, most profitable. Because of this, very good fish-catches can be enjoyed at low costs. The primary condition for this is the efficient functioning of rules.

14. There is much debate on the concept of maximum sustainable yield in fisheries, because it is extremely difficult to define the maximum catch without overusing the fish stock. This is due to the fact that one is unable to predict the exact fish population size, as this depends on the complex interactions in ecosystems (Becker and Ostrom 1995). Ostrom and Becker argue that it is, therefore, much better to analyze local strategies of resource use before making recommendations to local people (*ibid.*).

15. The perspective on institutions adopted here follows the approach of North (1990), who defines institutions as human-devised constraints that shape human interactions that ultimately affect the performance of an economy by their effects on the costs of exchange and production. In the context of common pool resource (CPR) management, institutions can be more specifically defined as a set of accepted social norms and rules for making decisions about resource use. These rules define who controls the resource, how conflicts are resolved, and how the resource is managed and exploited (Richards 1997).

16. See Fox (1983); Richards *et al.* (1999); Adhikari & Lovett (2000); Pretty *et. al.* (1995).

17. See Adhikari and Lovett (2005); Adhikari (2003).

18. UNHS – Uganda National Household Survey.

19. 'Christians' here included Roman Catholics, Anglicans and those belonging to a host of Evangelical and Pentecostal churches and denominations.

20. Chi-square = 12.943 $p< 0.227$

21. Exchange rate: US$ = 1620 Uganda Shillings at the time of the survey.

22. i.e. those households with the least amount of land attaching greater importance to community forests as a source of food or edible plants.

23. In fact, it is these actions of the very poor that appeared to underpin the pervasive skepticism some NFA officials had for community based organizations to engage local communities in CFM. Many of these officials viewed CFM as a mode of legitimizing illegal activities in community

forests. Thus, quite often CBO initiatives are perceived as luring communities to present CFM applications that do not have good intention for genuine partnerships for collaboration with the NFA. In addition, some communities think that an Agreement with NFA is a permit for undertaking unacceptable activities in the forests, and in this regard provide incentives for the most economically disadvantaged to engage in these activities (private communication with NFA officials)

24. Respondents were weary of admitting to marketing community forest products as such marketing could point to admitting to a host of illegal activities in the forests, especially charcoal burning.

25. In any case, whether one sees it from the point of view of reduced frequency of visits (i.e. households possess sufficient tools to efficiently harvest forest resources) or from the point of view of households not possessing sufficient tools and therefore having to pay more frequent visits to the forests; the statistical significance of the relations is implied.

26. It was difficult to attach monetary values to the other different forest products households procured from their community forests. For example, it was difficult to attach money values to key forest products such as herbs and medicinal plants and a host of edible plants, given households' use values for such products, which in the main were spiritual and/or traditional in nature.

27. See
http://www.unesco.org/water/wwap/wwdr/wwdr2/case_studies/pdf/uganda.pdf

28. It should be noted that most springs from which households collect water were improvised water holes, which afforded variable access to some resource extractors (i.e. children and women). In addition, some households were clearly located far from these water points, adding to resource transportation times. Nevertheless, the data as presented reveals very few households reporting resource appropriation costs in excess of Ugandan shillings 2000 and where this occurs, it is more significant with respect to productive asset holdings of middle wealth and rich households with threshold levels of tools whose values are amortized over time.

29. Also, CFM information (such as its contribution to livelihoods improvement, fuel wood, value for environmental conservation, contribution to rainfall and soil protection) is not reflected in government statistics. Therefore the importance and contribution of CFM to the gross development strategies of the communities and the country are underestimated. This undermines the significance of CFM to rural livelihoods especially for the forest dependant poor.

30. LC2 Chairman, Nyantonzi parish, Masindi District

31. Due to the diverse ethnic mix in the study communities the role traditional institutions of leadership play in influencing community members' use and

access to forest resources was not evident. However, Local Councils (LCs) were observed to be important in influencing community members use and access patterns in community forests.

32. Transaction Costs in Community Forestry Activities/Total Resource Appropriation Costs.
33. Transaction Costs in Community Forestry Activities/Total Benefits from Community Forests.

REFERENCES

Acharya, U., Petheram, R.J. and Reid, R. 2004. Concepts and perceptions of biodiversity in community forestry, Nepal, *Small-scale Forest Economics, Management and Policy*, 3(3): 401-410.

Acheson, James. 1989. Management of common-property resources. In: St. Plattner (ed.). *Economic Anthropology*. Standford: Standford Uniiversity Press, pp. 351-378.

Adams, W. M. 1990. *Green development. Environment and sustainability in the Third World.* London: Routledge.

Adhikari, B. 2003. Property rights and natural resource: socio-economic heterogeneity and distributional implications of common property resource management. *South Asian Network for Development and Environmental Economics Working Paper* 1-03, Kathmandu, Nepal.

_____. (forthcoming).Institutions and collective action: does heterogeneity matter in community-based resource management? *Journal of Development Studies*.

Adhikari, B. and Lovett, J.C. 2006. Transaction costs and community-based natural resource management in Nepal. J. *Enviromental Management* 78, 5–15.

Adhikari, B., Di Falco, S. and Lovett, J.C. 2004. Household characteristics and forest dependency: Evidence from community-based forest management in Nepal. *Ecological Economics* 48 (2), 245–257.

Aggarwal, R.M. 2000. Possibilities and limitations to cooperation in small groups: the case of group-owned wells in southern India. *World Development* 28 (8), 1481–1497.

Alaska Department of Natural Resources. 2004. Alaska community forestry programmme: What is community forestry? Division of forestry. Available from http://www.dnr.state.ak.us/forestry/community

Alchian, A.A. and Demsetz, H. 1972. Production, information costs, and economic organization. *American Economic Review*. 62, 777–795.

Alden, Wily. L. 1997. Villagers as forest managers and governments 'learning to let go' the case of Duru-Haitemba & Mgori forests in Tanzania No. 9 Forest Participation Series IIED (International Institute for Environment & Development), London.

_____. 1999. Moving forward in African community forestry: Trading power not use rights. *Society and Natural Resources*, Vol. 12:49-61, Wisconsin.

_____. 2000. The evolution of community based forest management in Tanzania. In *FAO 2000.*

_____. 2000. The democratisation of forest management in eastern and southern Africa. *International Forestry Review* 2 (4): 287-294, Oxford.

_____. 2001. Forest management and democracy in East and Southern Africa: Lessons from Tanzania. No. 95 Gatekeeper Series, IIED, London.

_____. 2003. Governance lessons from community forestry in Africa. Paper presented to the AFLEG Meeting of Ministers in Yaoundé, Cameroon, 12-16 October 2003. The World Bank.

Alden, Wily. L. and D. Hammond. 2001. Land security and the poor in Ghana. Is there a way forward. A land sector scoping study. DFID rural livelihoods programme, Accra.

Alden, Wily L. and P. Dewees. 2001. From users to custodians: Changing relations between people and the state in forest management in Tanzania. Work Bank Policy Research Paper 2569. 2001.

Alden, Wily. L. and Sue Mbaya. 2001. Land, people and forests in eastern & southern Africa at the beginning of the 21st Century. The impact of land relations of the role of communities in forest future. IUCN-EARO (monograph). 2001.

Apte, T. and Pathak, N. 2002. Learning lessons from international community forestry networks in India. Paper prepared for the CIFOR Project Learning from International Community Forestry Networks, Center for International Forestry Research, Bogor, http://www.cifor.cgiar.org/publications/pdf_files/CF/India_CF.pdf.

Asare, A. 1998. A report on community boundary maintenance contracts in forest reserves. CFMU, Kumasi.

Babin, D. and A. Bertrand. 1998. Managing pluralism: Subsidiarity and patrimonial mediation. In *Unasylva* No. 194: 19-25.

Baland, J. and Platteau, J. 1996. *Halting degradation of natural resources: Is there a role of rural communities*? Oxford University Press and FAO, Oxford, Rome.

Bardhan, P. 1993. Symposium on management of local commons. *Journal of Economic Perspectives* 7 (4), 87–92.

Becker, Dustin, C. and Elinor Ostrom. 1995. Human ecology and Resource Sustainability: The Importance of Institutional Diversity. *Annual Review of Ecololgy and Systematics* No. 26:113-33.

Benham, A. and Benham, L. 2000. Measuring the transaction costs. In: Menard, C. (ed.), *Institutions, contracts and organizations: Perspectives from new institutional economics*. Cheltenham: Edward Elgar Publishing,pp. 367–375.

Birner, R. and Wittmer, H. 2000. Co-management of natural resources: a transaction cost economic approach to determine the efficient boundary of the state. International Symposium of New Institutional Economics, 22–24

September 2000, Tubingen, Germany, Available at http://www.isnie.org/ISNIE00/finalprogram.htm # Panel 4A.

Boyd, C., Jones, B., Anstey S., S. Shackleton and C. Fabricus. 2001. Sustainable livelihoods in Southern Africa: Institutions, governance and policy processes. Wild Resources Theme Paper. SLSA Working Paper 5.

Bray, D.B., L. Merino-Perez, P. Negreros-Castillo, G. Segura-Warnholtz, J. Torres-Rojo and H. Vester. 2003. Mexico's community managed forests as a global model for sustainable landscapes. *Conservation Biology* Vol. 17, No. 3; 672-677.

Bromley, D. W. 1991. *Environment and economy: Property rights and public policy*. Oxford, UK, Oxford University Press.

_____. (ed.). 1992. *Making the commons work. Theory, practice, and policy*. San Francisco: ICS Press.

Bromley, D.W.and Cernea, M.M. 1989. The management of common property resources: Some conceptual and operational fallacies World Bank Discussion Paper. The World Bank, Washington, DC.

Campbell, B., A. Mandando, N. Nemarundwe, W. Jong, M. Luckret, and F. Matose. 2001. Challenges to proponents of common property resource systems: Despairing voices from the social forests of Zimbabwe. *World Development*, Vol. 29 (4) pp: 589-600.

Campbell, B., N. Byron, P. Hobane, P., F. Matose, F. Madzudzo and E. Alden Wily. 1999. Moving to local control of woodland resources –Can CAMPFIRE go beyond the Mega-Fauna? *Society and Natural Resources,* 12: 501-509.

Cheung, S.N. 1983. The contractual nature of the firm. *Journal of Law and Economics*, Vol. 26, pp: 1-22.

Cleaver, Frances. 2001. Institutions, agency and the limitations of participatory approaches to development. In: Cooke, B. and U. Kothari. (eds.). *Participation: The new tyranny*. New York: Zed Books. Pp: 36-55.

Coase, R. 1960. The problem of social cost. *Journal of Law and Economics* 3, 1–44.

Colchester, M., Apte, T., Laforge, M. and Pathak, N. 2003. Bridging the gap: Communities, forests and international networks. CIFOR Occasional Paper No. 41, Center for International Forestry Research, Bogor.

Coleman, J. 1990. *Foundations of social theory*. Cambridge, MA: Belknap Press.

Community Forestry Development Programme. 2003. *Database in Community Forestry in Nepal*. Department of Forest, Kathmandu, Nepal.

Crocker, T.D. 1971. Externalities, property rights and transactions costs: An empirical study. *Journal of Law and Economics* 14, 451–464.

Cross River State Community Forestry Project (CRSCFP). 2001. *Mission statement*. Calabar, Nigeria.

Davies, J. and Richards, M. 1999. The use of economics to assess stakeholder's incentives in participatory forest management: A review European Union Tropical Forestry Paper, vol. 5. London: Overseas Development Institute,

Denman Community Forest Cooperative. 2004, Directory of community forest organisations of British Columbia. Available from http://www.denmanis.bc.ca/directory/index.html.

Dubois, O. and J. Lowore. 2000. The journey towards collaborative forest management in Africa: Lessons and some navigational aids. Forestry and Land Use Series No. 15. London: IIED.

Ebner, R. 1996. Local knowledge of trees among the Bhil in Southern Rajasthan: with special reference to its value and implications for rural development. Working Paper No. 96/4, Department of Forest Sciences, Swiss Federal Institute of Technology, Zurich.

Emtage, N.F. 2004. Stakeholder's roles and responsibilities in the Community-Based Forest Management Programme of the Philippines, *Small-scale Forest Economics, Management and Policy*, 3(3): 319-336.

Ensminger, Jean. 1992. *Making a market. The institutional transformation of an African society*. Cambridge: Cambridge University Press.

Ensminger, Jean. 1998. Anthropology and the new institutionalism. *Journal of Institutional and Theoretical Economics (JITE)*, vol. 154:774-789.

Estoria, E.; Herbohn, J. L. and Harrison, S. R. 2004. The performance of community organizers in promotion of community forestry in Leyte Province, Philippines, *Small-scale Forest Economics, Management and Policy*, 3(3): 363-384.

Fairhead, James and Leach, Melissa. 1996. *Misreading the African landscape. Society and ecology in a forest-savanna mosaic*. Cambridge:Cambridge University Press.

Falconer, K. 2000. Farm-level constraints on agri-environmental scheme participation: A transactional perspective. *Journal of Rural Studies* 16, 379–394.

Farm Africa. 2000. Phase II Kafa-Sheka Project Proposal. Addis Ababa: Farm Ethiopia-Farm Africa.

Food and Agriculture Organization (FAO). 1978. Forestry for local community development. Forestry Paper No. 7, Rome: FAO Forestry Department.

_____. 2000. Proceedings of the First International Workshop on Community Forestry in Africa. Rome.

_____. 2001. *State of the world's forests 2001*.

_____. 2002. Law and sustainable development since Rio. Legal trends in agriculture and natural resource management. FAO Legislative Study, 73.FAO.

_____. 2003. Proceedings of the Second International Workshop on Participatory Forestry in Africa. Rome.

Forestry and Beekeeping Division, Ministry of Natural Resources & Environment. Government of Tanzania (FBD). 2001. Guideline for establishing community based forest management. Dar es Salaam.

_____.. 1998. Community forestry implementing guidelines. Banjul, The Gambia.

Federation of Community Forestry Users (FECOFUN). 2004. What's new [?]. Available from http://www.fecofun.org

Feeney, D. *et al.* 1990. The tragedy of the commons: Twenty-two years later. *Human Ecology* 18, 1:1-19.

Fenoaltea, S. 1984. Slavery and supervision in comparative perspectives: A model. *Journal of Economic History* 44, 635–668.

Filimao, E., E. Mansur and L. Namanha. 2000. Tchuma Tchato: An evolving experience of community based natural resource management in Mozambique.In FAO 2000.

Fomete, T. 2001. The forestry taxation system and the involvement of local communities in forest management in Cameroon. ODI RDFM Paper No. 25b.

Fox, J.M. 1983. Managing public lands in a subsistence economy: The perspective from a Nepali village. Unpublished PhD Dissertation. University of Wisconsin-Madison.

Gardner, A., J. DeMarco and C. Asanga. 2001. A conservation partnership: Community forestry at Kilum-Ijim. ODI Rural Development Forestry Network Paper No.25.

Gerrits, R.V. 1996. The Philippine government's approach to upland development: The Integrated Social Forestry Programme, SEARCA-UQ Uplands Research Project Working Paper No. 16, Los Baños.

Gibson, Clarke, C. 1999. *Politicians and poachers. The political economy of wildlife policy in Africa.* Cambridge: Cambridge University Press.

Government of Uganda (GoU). 2001. The 2001 Forestry Policy. Ministry of Water Lands and Environmen

_____. 2002. The national forest plan 2002. Ministry of water, Land and the Environment.

Gregorio, N.; Herbohn, J.L. and Harrison, S.R. 2004. Small-scale forestry development in Leyte, Philippines: The central role of nurseries, *Small-scale Forest Economics, Management and Policy*, 3(3): 337-351.

Hanna, S. 1995. Efficiencies of user participation in natural resource management. In: Hanna, S. and Munasinghe, M. (eds.). *Property rights and the environment: Social and ecological issues.* Washington, DC.: The Beijer International Institute of Ecological Economics and The World Bank.

Hardin, Garret. 1968. The tragedy of the Commons. *Science* 162: 1243–48.

Harrison, S.R.; Emtage, N. F. and Nasayao, E.E. 2004. Past and present forestry support programmes in the Philippines, and lessons for the future. *Small-scale Forest Economics, Management and Policy*, 3(3): 303-317.

Harrison, S.R.; Ghose, A.S. and Herbohn, J.L. 2001. Lessons from social and community forestry in the Tropics, with particular reference to India and the Philippines. In S.R. Harrison and J.L. Herbohn (eds), *Sustainable farm forestry in the Tropics.* Cheltenham: Edward Elgar, pp. 227-240.

Hartebrodt, C.; Fillibrandt, T. and Brandl, H. 2005. Community forests in Baden-Wurttemberg: A case study in successful public/public partnership. *Small-scale Forestry,* Vol. 4 No.3. pp. 229-250.

Helms, J.A. (ed.). 1998. The dictionary of forestry. Bethesda and Wallingford: The society of American foresters and CABI Publishing.

Hesse, C. and P. Trench. 2000. Decentralisation and institutional survival of the fittest in the Sahel –what hope CPRM? Paper presented at the Eighth Biennial Conference of the International Association for the Study of Common Property, Bloomington, Indiana, 29 May -4 June 2000.

Hobley, M. and Wollenberg, E. 1996. A new pragmatic forestry or another development bandwagon. In: Hobley, M. (ed.). *Participatory forestry: The process of change in India and Nepal. Rural development forestry study guide 3.* London: Overseas Development Institute, pp. 243–260.

Holloway, G.; Nicholson, C.; Delgado, C.; Staal, S. and Ehui, S. 2000. Agroindustrialization through institutional innovation: transaction costs, cooperatives, and milk-market development in the east-African highlands. *Agricultural Economics* 23, 279–288.

Iddi, S. 2000. Community involvement in forest management: First experiences from Tanzania. The Gologolo Joint Forest Management Project: A case study from the West Usambaras Mountains. In FAO 2000a.

Jones, B.T. 1999. Community management of natural resources in Namibia. Issue Paper No. 90, London: IIED.

Kellert, S. R; Mehta, J. N; Ebbin, S. A. and Lichtenfeed, L.L. 2000. Community natural resource management: Promise, rhetoric, and reality, *Society and Natural Resources*, vol. 13, pp. 705-15.

Kerkhof, P. 2000. *Local forest management in the Sahel. Towards a new social contract.* SOS Sahel.

Klein, M.; Salla B. and H. Kok. 2001. Attempts to establish community forests in Lomie, Cameroon. ODI RDFN Paper No. 25f.

Kubsa, A. 2002. Granting exclusive user rights to the forest dwellers in the state owned forest: The WAJIB approach in Ethiopia. Paper presented to the Second International Workshop on Participatory Forest Management in Africa held in Arusha Tanzania, 18-22 February 2002.

Kumm, K.I. and Drake, L. 1998. Transaction costs to farmers of environmental compensation. Unpublished Report, Department of Economics, SLU, University of Uppsala, Sweden.

Kuperan, K.; Mustapha, N.; Abdullah, R.; Pomeroy, R.S.; Genio, E. and Salamanca, A. 1998. Measuring transaction costs of fisheries co-management. Paper Presented at the Seventh Biennial Conference of the International Association for the Study of Common Property, Vancouver. Canada. Available at: http://www.indiana.edu/~iasap/Drafts/kuperan.pdf

Lawbuary, J. 2004. Eucalyptus planting in social forestry in India: Boon or curse?' Available at: http://www.ganesha.co.uk/Articles/Eucalyptus.htm,

Leffler, K. and Rucker, R. 1991. Transaction costs and the efficient organization of production: A study of timber harvesting contracts. *Journal of Political Economy* 99, 1060–1087.

Lukama, B. 2000. Participatory forest management: A strategy for sustainable forest management in Africa. A case study of the Chinyunyu Community Forestry Project, Zambia. In FAO 2000.

Makarabhirom, P. 2004. Fatal struggle for Thailand's community forests. *Bulletin of the Global Caucus on Community Based Forest Management,* Fall 2004 issue, pp. 1, 15.

Malla, Y. B; Hari, R. N and Branney, P. J. 2003. Why aren't poor people benefiting more from community forestry? *Journal of Forest and Livelihood*, vol. 3, no. 1, pp. 78-92.

Malla, Y.B. 2000. Impact of community forestry policy on rural livelihood and food security in Nepal. *Unasylva* 51, 37-45.

Mangaoang, E.O. and Cedamon, E.D. 2004. Building-up partnerships for community forestry: The ACIAR Smallholder Forestry Project experience, *Small-scale Forest Economics, Management and Policy*, 3(3): 353-362.

Mauambeta, D. 2000. Sustainable management of indigenous forests in Mwanza East, Malawi. In FAO 2000.

Mayers, J.; Evans, J. and T. Foy. 2001. Raising the stakes – Impacts of privatisation, certification and partnerships in South African forestry. London: IIED.

Mburu, J.; Birner, R. and Zeller, M. 2003. Relative importance and determinants of landowners transaction costs in collaborative wildlife management in Kenya: An empirical analysis. *Ecological Economics* 45, 59–73.

Ministry of Environment and Forests (MINEF). 1998. Manual of the procedures for the attribution, norms and management of community forests. Government of Cameroon.

Molians, J. R. 1998. The impact of inequality, gender, external assistance and social capital on local-level collective action. *World Development* 26 (3), 413–431.

Nana, A. (2000). An example of cooperation between government and non-government institutions in carrying out community forest management activities. The Case of Naturama's activities in the Kabore Tambi National Park in Bukina Faso. In FAO 2000.

National Community Forest Partnership. 2004. Environmental regeneration – shaping the future. Available at: http://www.communityforest.org.uk/

Negrao, J. 1998. Land reform and community-based natural resource management in Mozambique. Ch. 2 ZERO-REO.

North, D.C. 1990. *Institutions, institutional change and economic performance.* Cambridge: Cambridge University Press.

Nugent, J.B. 1993. Between state, markets and households: A neo institutional analysis of local organizations and institutions. *World Development* 21 (4), 623–632.

Oakerson, R.J. 1992. Analysing the commons: A framework. In: Bromley, D.W. (ed.), *Making the Commons work: Theory, practice, and policy.* San Francisco:. ICS press.

Olsson, O. 1999. A Microeconomic analysis of institutions. Working Paper in Economics No. 25, Department of Economics, Goteborg University.

Ostrom, E. 1990. Governing the Commons: The evolution of institutions for collective action. Cambridge: Cambridge University Press.

_____. 1994. Constituting social capital and collective action. *Journal of Theoretical Politics* 6 (4), 527–562.

Pennsylvania Urban and Community Forestry Council. 2004. Available from: http://www.dcnr.state.pa.us/forestry/pucfc/

Prasad, R. and Bhatanagar, P. 1995. *Social forestry experiences over a decade.*, Dehra Dun: International Book Distributors.

Pretty, J.N.; Guijt, I.; Thompson, J. and Scoones, I. 1995. *Participatory learning and action; A trainer's guide.* London: International Institute for Environment and Development.

Republic of Uganda, Ministry of Water, Lands and Environment. 2001. The 2001 forestry policy.

_____. 2002. The national forest plan.

Ribot, J. 1999. Decentralisation, participation and accountability in Sahelian forestry: Legal instruments of political-administrative control. In *Africa* 69 (1): 23-64.

Richards, M.; K. Kanel, M. Maharjan and J. Davies. 1999. Towards participatory economic analysis by forest user groups in Nepal. ODI, Portland House, Stag Place, London, UK.

Roberts, E.H. and Gautam, M.K. 2003. *Community forestry lessons for Australia: A review of international case studies.* School of Resources, Environment and Society, Australian National University, Canberra.

Ruttan, Lore M. 1998. Closing the commons: Cooperation for gain or restraint? *Human Ecology*, Vol. 26, No. 1, 1998: 43-66.

Saarela-Kaonga, T. 2001. Community forestry in cross river state of Nigeria. Lessons learnt and the way forward. Nigeria: Living Earth Foundation.

Sarre, A. 1994. What is community forestry? *Tropical Forest Update*, 4(4): 2.

Saxena, N.C. 1989. *Degraded lands in India, problems and prospects.* Bangkok, FAO.

Stamm, V. 2000. The rural land Plan: An innovative approach from Cote D'Ivoire. Issue Paper No. 91, IIED.

Tang, S.Y. 1992. *Institutions and collective action: Self-governing in irrigation systems.* ICS Press, San Francisco.

Texier, J. (n.d). Trends in forestry law in Europe and Africa. *Legislative Study* No. 72. Rome: FAO.

Tanzania Forest Conservation Group (TFCG). 2001. *The Arc Journal,* No. 12 (August).

Treue, T. 2004. History of community forestry. Unpublished lecture notes. Available from: http://www.kursus.kvl.dk/shares/cf/300_materials/CF%20History%201.ppt, The Royal Veterinary and Agricultural University, Denmark.

Uganda Forest Department (UFD). 2000. Collaborative forest management agreement between the forest department and Bumusili village regarding the management of Namatale forest reserve, Kampala.

Uphoff, N. 1993. Grassroots organization and NGOs in rural development: opportunities with diminishing states and expanding markets. *World Development* 21 (4), 607–622.

US Federal Forest Service. 2004. Technical guide to urban and community forestry: Values of Urban Trees. Available from:http://www.na.fs.fed.us/spfo/pubs/uf/techquide/values.htm

Veer, C. 2004. Community-based forest management in Asia: quo vadis? *Bulletin of the Global Caucus on Community Based Forest Management*, Fall issue, p. 12.

Vudzijena, V. 1998. Land reform and community based natural resource management in Zimbabwe in ZERO-REO, Ch. 5.

Wade, R. 1988. Village republics: Economic conditions for collective Action in South India. Cambridge: Cambridge University Press.

Wang, S. and van Kooten, G. C. 1999. Silvicultural contracting in British Columbia: A transaction cost economics approach. *Forest Science* 45 (2), 272–279.

Washington Department of Natural Resources. 2004. Urban and community forestry programme. Available from: http://www.dnr.wa.gov/htdocs/rp/urban/urban.htm,

White, R. 1998. Land issues and land reform in Botswana in ZERO-REO, Ch. 1.

Wild, R. and J. Mutebi. 1996. Conservation through community use of plant resources. Establishing collaborative management at Bwindi Impenetrable and Mgahinga Gorilla National Parks, Uganda. Working Paper No. 5 of People and Plants Programme, UNESCO, Paris.

Williamson, O.E. 1991. Comparative economic organization: The analysis of discrete structural alternatives. *Administrative Science Quarterly* 36 (2), 269–296.

Wily, L. A. 2003. Participatory forest management in Africa: An overview of progress and issues. Paper presented at the Second International Workshop on Participatory Forestry in Africa.

_____. 2004. Can we really own the forest? A critical examination of tenure development in community forestry in Africa. Paper presented at The Tenth Biennial Conference, International Association for the Study of Common Property (IASCP), Oaxaca, Mexico, August 9-13.

World Rainforest Movement. 2004. Towards community forestry in Indonesia. Available from: http://www.wrm.org.uy/bulletin/63/Indonesia.html.

Xu, J., Zhao, Y. and Suh, J. 2004. Community forestry for poverty alleviation in China with reference to Huoshan County, Anhui Province, *Small-scale Forest Economics, Management and Policy*, 3(3): 385-400.

Zak, P.J. and Knack, S. 2001. Trust and growth. *The Economic Journal* 111 (470), 295–321.

Zhang, Y. 2000. Costs of plan versus costs of markets: Reforms in China's state-owned forest management. *Development Policy Review* 18 (3), 285–306.

_____. 2001. Economics of transaction costs saving forestry. *Ecological Economics* 36, 197–204.